C000061508

A Practice of Padmasambhava

A Practice of Padmasambhava

ESSENTIAL INSTRUCTIONS ON THE PATH TO AWAKENING

by Shechen Gyaltsap IV and Rinchen Dargye

Foreword by Chökyi Nyima Rinpoche

Translated by the Dharmachakra Translation Committee

SNOW LION PUBLICATIONS

ITHACA, NEW YORK

Snow Lion Publications
P.O. Box 6483
Ithaca, NY 14851 USA
(607) 273-8519
www.snowlionpub.com

Printed in USA on acid-free recycled paper.

Painting of Vādisiṃha on p. 166 from the personal collection of
Orgyen Tobgyal Rinpoche, photo copyright Rigpa International.
Drawings on pp. 16 and 100 by Chris Banigan.
Designed and typeset by Gopa & Ted2, Inc.

ISBN-10: 1-55939-362-9
ISBN-13: 978-1-55939-362-1

Library of Congress Cataloging-in-Publication Data

A practice of Padmasambhava : essential instructions on the path to awakening / by Shechen Gyaltsap IV and Rinchen Dargye ; foreword by Chökyi Nyima Rinpoche ; translated by the Dharmachakra Translation Committee.
p. cm.
Includes translations from Tibetan.
Includes bibliographical references.
ISBN-13: 978-1-55939-362-1 (alk. paper)
ISBN-10: 1-55939-362-9 (alk. paper)
1. Spiritual life—Tantric Buddhism. 2. Padma Sambhava, ca. 717-ca. 762.
3. Mchog-gyur-gliṅ-pa, Gter-ston, 1829-1870. Bla ma'i thugs sgrub bar chad kun sel. I. Chökyi Nyima, Rinpoche, 1951- II. Źe-chen rgyal-tshab padma-'gyur-med-rnam-rgyal, 1871-1926. Thugs sgrub bar chad kun sel gyi rim pa daṅ po'i khrid kyi zin bris lha rdzas me tog. English. III. Karma-rin-chen-dar-rgyas, Mkhan-po. Bla ma smra ba'i seṅ ge'i phrin las blo gros dpal ster gyi rnam bśad rab gsal snaṅ ba. English. IV. Dharmachakra Translation Committee.
BQ7690.P73 2011
294.3'444—dc22 2010032835

Contents

Foreword by Chökyi Nyima Rinpoche . . . vii

Translators' Introduction . . . 1

Acknowledgments . . . 13

Divine Flower: A Guide to the First Level of Practice of "Accomplishing the Guru's Mind: Dispeller of All Obstacles," by Shechen Gyaltsap Pema Namgyal . . . 15

Brilliant Light: A Commentary on the Activity of Guru Vādisiṃha That Bestows the Glory of Intelligence, by Karma Rinchen Dargye . . . 99

Blooming Intelligence: The Practice Manual of Guru Vādisiṃha . . . 165

Bibliography . . . 177

Foreword by Chökyi Nyima Rinpoche

PADMASAMBHAVA, the second buddha, is a kind and loving protector for all of us sentient beings. In particular, through his enlightened activity, the Buddha's teaching spread to the snowy land of Tibet where, like the sun shining in the sky, it became a source of happiness and awakening for countless practitioners.

While in Tibet, Padmasambhava concealed many of his teachings as spiritual treasures, meant to benefit future disciples. One of the masters who discovered these teachings was the great treasure revealer Chokgyur Dechen Shigpo Lingpa. An undisputed emissary of Padmasambhava, the treasures that he revealed contain a swift path to perfect and complete enlightenment. Fortunately, all of these teachings are still with us and available to anyone who seeks to awaken to enlightenment within this very life.

However, to engage in these practices, it is necessary to first meet a qualified master and receive the ripening empowerments, the supportive reading transmissions, and the liberating oral instructions. Having obtained such preparatory training, the student must then diligently put the teachings into practice. At that point, the instruction manuals composed by learned and accomplished masters to elucidate key points of meditation practice can become a true guide to one's progress on the path.

For this reason, I am pleased to present two important commentaries on the practice of Padmasambhava according to Chokgyur Lingpa's profound treasure, *Accomplishing the Guru's Mind: Dispeller of All Obstacles.* These texts, which were prepared by the Dharmachakra Translation Committee, are composed by two of the great masters in the lineage. *Divine Flower* by Shechen Gyaltsap Pema Namgyal skillfully guides practitioners through the preliminaries and the main part of practice according to the general principles of *Accomplishing the Guru's Mind.* In contrast, *Brilliant Light* by Karmey Khenpo Rinchen Dargye, a direct disciple of the great treasure revealer himself, presents specific advice and guidance for the practice of Guru Vādisiṃha, the wisdom aspect of Padmasambhava according to this same cycle of teachings.

It is my wish that these texts will be of benefit for all practitioners of secret mantra who aspire to the accomplishments of the Lotus-Born Guru. May the merit that arises from this publication be a cause for the enlightenment of all beings, as far as space pervades.

Translators' Introduction

IN THIS VOLUME, the reader will find translations of two commentaries on the practice of the enlightened teacher, Padmasambhava. This great master, also known as Guru Rinpoche, is accredited with establishing the Buddhist tantric teaching in Tibet during the golden age in the ninth century, a time when Buddhism benefited from a strong royal patronage. According to traditional accounts, during his Tibetan sojourn, Padmasambhava concealed numerous spiritual treasures, destined for revelation at later times. These concealed teachings would subsequently be discovered by a great number of extraordinary masters, or treasure revealers as they were called, who upheld Padmasambhava's legacy and propagated his teachings to practitioners in all the regions of Tibet. Both of the texts presented in this volume are rooted in, and draw their inspiration from, the revelations of the treasure revealer Chokgyur Lingpa (1829–1870), in particular his most influential revelation, the scriptural collection known as *Accomplishing the Guru's Mind: Dispeller of All Obstacles* (*Bla ma'i thugs sgrub bar chad kun sel*).

The first of the two commentaries, *Divine Flower* (*Thugs sgrub bar chad kun sel gyi rim pa dang po'i khrid kyi zin bris lha rdzas me tog*), was composed by Shechen Gyaltsap Gyurme Pema Namgyal (1871–1926) and provides a detailed commentary on *Accomplishing the Guru's Mind* as a whole, treating both the preliminaries and the main part of practice. In contrast, the second text, *Brilliant Light* (*Bla ma smra ba'i seng ge'i phrin las blo gros dpal ster gyi rnam bshad rab gsal snang ba*), composed by Karma Rinchen Dargye (b. 1835), focuses on just one emanation of Padmasambhava, namely, Guru Vādisiṃha (or Lama Mawey Senge, as he is known in Tibet). Although this text is concerned with a particular aspect of Padmasambhava, most of its explanations and instructions are equally applicable to other practice manuals from *Accomplishing the Guru's Mind* and also the practice of the development stage as a whole.

As such, the two texts complement each other well and together provide a good introduction to the practices associated with this popular cycle of treasure teachings. As these precious texts are best studied in the company of an authentic master of the lineage, we highly encourage readers of this book to receive the proper explanations and transmissions related to these texts from a qualified lineage master. Therefore we shall here refer any philosophical and practical questions on the content of the commentaries to the relevant authorities and instead limit ourselves to a few observations on the historical context of the tradition to which the translations belong.

Chokgyur Lingpa and *The New Treasures*

Chokgyur Lingpa, who revealed the treasure practices that concern this book, was born in the fall of 1829 at the retreat center of Gomde Dranang, situated in the eastern Tibetan region of Dokham. His father was the mantra adept Pema Wangchuk and his mother the practitioner Tsering Yangtso. We are told that, born amid auspicious signs of rainbow lights, he grew up to become an intelligent child who would naturally engage in meditation practice without formal training or prompting. At the age of eleven he experienced his first vision of Padmasambhava, which sparked the beginning of a long and fruitful career as a treasure revealer. The young Chokgyur Lingpa revealed his first treasure later that same year. Around this time he took novice vows, but it was not until later in life that he met his principal teachers. Thus, in 1853 at the age of twenty-four, Chokgyur Lingpa connected with Jamgön Kongtrul Lodrö Thaye (1813–1899) and Jamyang Khyentse Wangpo (1820–1892), the great masters of his day with whom he was to develop a lifelong relationship.

At this time Chokgyur Lingpa had already revealed several of his many treasures, including *Accomplishing the Guru's Mind: Dispeller of All Obstacles*, which he discovered in 1848. When Chokgyur Lingpa later showed this treasure to Khyentse Wangpo, he discovered that Khyentse had revealed an almost identical treasure himself and so their mutual respect was consolidated. According to Tulku Urgyen (1920–1996), Khyentse subsequently burned his treasure, saying "Since the words and the meaning are identical, what is the use of having two! Yours, being an earth treasure is more profound and will be more effectual than my mind treasure" (Erik Pema Kunsang and Marcia Binder Schmidt, *Blazing Splendor: The Memoirs of Tulku Urgyen Rinpoche* [Hong Kong: Rangjung Yeshe Publications, 2005], 42–43). In this way Chokgyur Lingpa's earth treasure, being a physical revelation, was considered more valuable than the immaterial mind treasure that Khyentse had discovered.

Chokgyur Lingpa's relationship with Khyentse and Kongtrul was a major influence on his life and treasure revelations, and it is clear that both of these extraordinary masters in turn also considered Chokgyur Lingpa their teacher, as both were actively involved in propagating his revelations. Often they would act as his scribe, recording the words dictated as he deciphered the script on the yellow scrolls of his treasure revelations. Both masters were also deeply involved in the ecumenical tradition that flourished in eastern Tibet at the time, and consequently Chokgyur Lingpa became an active participant in that movement as well.

Throughout his career as a treasure revealer, Chokgyur Lingpa revealed mostly earth treasures, apparently in respect of advice from Situpa Pema Nyinche Wangpo (1774–1853) to keep his mind treasures secret. Over time, as many of his treasures were revealed in public and enjoyed the support of Khyentse and Kongtrul, Chokgyur Lingpa became a well-respected treasure revealer with considerable influence on many Buddhist lineages. Sadly, however, although the life of Chokgyur Lingpa was full of great accomplishments, he did not live long. On June 29, 1870, at the young age of forty, we are told that Chokgyur Lingpa had a vision of journeying to a pure buddha field and subsequently passed away amid various miraculous signs.

The *New Treasures of Chokgyur Lingpa* (*Mchog gling gter gsar*) contains his many revelations as well as the surrounding commentarial literature by many masters of the lineage. These texts were first compiled by the second incarnation of Chokgyur Lingpa in the Kela lineage, Konchog Gyurmey Tenpey Gyaltsen (1875?–1938?). Although barely 150 years old, the revelations from the *New Treasures* have had a great influence on both the Nyingma and the Kagyu schools of Tibetan Buddhism up to the present day. This collection, which comprises both Chokgyur Lingpa's treasures and their commentaries, has continued to grow and presently contains an impressive forty volumes. The works included in the *New Treasures*, apart from the revealed treasures themselves, represent a variety of literary genres by authors such as Khyentse, Kongtrul, the fourteenth and fifteenth Karmapas, subsequent Chokling incarnations, and other lineage holders, such as Rinchen Dargye and Shechen Gyaltsap IV.

More specifically, the teachings contained in *Accomplishing the Guru's Mind: Dispeller of All Obstacles* make up the first nine and a half volumes of the *New Treasures*. The practices found in this cycle are focused on the outer principle of the guru, identified according to the structure of the three bodies of enlightenment as Amitāyus (the dharma body), Avalokiteśvara (the enjoyment body), and Padmasambhava (the emanation body). Moreover, at the level of the emanation body, twelve manifestations of Padmasambhava are found in this cycle, among whom the second is Guru Vādisiṃha, who is the subject of the commentary in *Brilliant Light*.

The root tantra of the cycle, *The Essence Manual of Oral Instructions*, contains the key practices for all these deities, while the surrounding scriptures unpack these teachings for practical use by the practitioner in the form of preliminary practices and instructions on the implementation of the practice manuals. The main practice manual for Padmasambhava in this cycle is found in four versions ranging from the very brief to the highly elaborate. In addition, we also find separate practice manuals for each of the twelve manifestations, such as that of Guru Vādisiṃha, which is translated in this volume. The collection additionally includes practices for the four classes of ḍākas and ḍākinīs related to the cycle, as well as a variety of rituals, empowerment guidelines, protector practices, and commentaries on the various aspects of practice. In this way, the teachings in *Accomplishing the Guru's Mind* represent a complete path to awakening.

Divine Flower by Shechen Gyaltsap IV

In *Divine Flower*, Shechen Gyaltsap guides the practitioner through the entire path as it is presented in *Accomplishing the Guru's Mind*. The text will be of great interest to practitioners who want to understand more deeply the internal logic of the Buddhist path in the Tibetan tradition. While it primarily provides an overview of the so-called preliminaries according to this particular tradition, the author contextualizes the classic hundred thousand accumulation practices within the wider scope of the Buddhist path. Why do we do the preliminaries? Where do they lead us? Shechen Gyaltsap shows how these questions tap into deeper questions about why we do spiritual practice.

What does it mean to have a precious human life? How can we make use of it when we have no idea how long it will last? What is the use of trying to be good? What is the difference between the fleeting happiness that constantly slips through our fingers and true contentment? Whether one is a newcomer to Tibetan Buddhism considering taking a step onto its path or an old hand at meditation practice, the four reflections that Shechen Gyaltsap lays out on the preciousness of human life, impermanence, karma, and the ultimately dissatisfying quality of life are sure to inspire us to take hold of our lives.

A scholar in the best possible sense, he leads us through the lush topographies of the traditional Buddhist universe with all its human and nonhuman beings, while again and again making appeals to direct human experience; in doing so, he points out the truths common to all of life. Along the way unfold poignant discussions on ethics and causality, for which *Divine Flower* serves as a noteworthy representation of Buddhist viewpoints. Readers will be pleased by Shechen Gyaltsap's incorporation of the Buddha's first teaching, the four truths, into the mix and will see how in fact the Tibetan preliminaries are founded on them as well.

Thus, by the time we reach the actual practice of the preliminaries, beginning with refuge, we have arrived at a sense of why we are here. At this point, Shechen Gyaltsap embarks on a descriptive journey into the introductory practices of *Accomplishing the Guru's Mind*. Little of the information he presents is unique to this cycle, however. He chooses not to delve completely into the characteristically elaborate visualizations associated with each practice and instead devotes the majority of his explanations toward fleshing out the theory behind the practices, which is common to any specific version of the preliminaries.

In much the same way as Patrul Rinpoche's (1808–1887) well-known guidance text, *The Words of My Perfect Teacher*, Shechen Gyaltsap provides a practical outline for practitioners to connect with the vajra vehicle, showing how each aspect of the trainings builds on the preceding practices. He also shows how each one serves as a jumping-off point into meditation on the nature of mind. Like Patrul, he demonstrates the deep roots the preliminaries have in Buddhism in general, making repeated references to sūtras as well as classic Indian works such as *The Way of the Bodhisattva*. The preliminaries are in fact advanced methods for clearing away the obscurations of mind and accumulating spiritual merit. The commentary on guru yoga in its outer, inner, and innermost aspects provides an exceptionally lucid introduction to the tantric Buddhist principle of guru devotion.

After this, Shechen Gyaltsap chooses to go further than Patrul Rinpoche and to offer guidance into the main vajra vehicle practices of development and completion stage meditation. He commences with a general survey of visualization techniques and the structures of the practice, which in itself can stand alone as an introduction to the complex world of the development stage. As he then gradually paints a portrait of the maṇḍala of *Accomplishing the Guru's Mind*—Padmasambhava with his twelve manifestations, including Vādisiṃha—he shows how a maṇḍala arises out of emptiness as the expression of wisdom and compassion. His lengthy description of the meaning behind each and every aspect of the images in the section on "Recollecting Purity" is especially valuable in shedding light on the mysterious esoteric symbolism that is so rife in development stage practice. He concludes by giving a pith instruction on the essence of mind, which poetically crystallizes the intent of all the other practices, and which could very well serve as the basis for an oral teaching on the Great Perfection in is own right.

All this while Shechen Gyaltsap intersperses practical comments for practitioners, which he uses to point out how every aspect—from reflecting on the truth of suffering to resting in the nature of mind—can be combined within one single session. In this way, his text follows the traditional approach of the Indian masters in outlining a way to attain enlightenment based on a single deity. *Divine Flower* thus serves as a guidebook for beginners and experienced students alike, a map of the path from beginning to end. It will be of great value to those of us in need of such a map, providing as it does rich and lucid explanations of the rationale and symbolism behind the core practices of the vajra vehicle and showing how the entire path opens up into the Great Perfection.

Shechen Gyaltsap Pema Namgyal was a disciple of the two towering masters of the nineteenth century, Jamyang Khyentse Wangpo and Jamgön Kongtrul. Recognized as the incarnation of the third Shechen Gyaltsap, he studied under many of the great masters of his day. Although he inherited the responsibilities for the famous Nyingma monastery of Shechen in East Tibet, at the age of twenty he underwent a spiritual transformation while on pilgrimage and subsequently elected to spend the majority of his remaining life in retreat. There, he practiced wholeheartedly while nonetheless becoming a prolific author. His collected works now fill thirteen volumes and cover a wide range of topics, from astrology to grammar, and almost every aspect of Buddhist doctrine. Having passed away at a young age, he did not live to see the turmoil of the 1950s, but nonetheless mentored many of the great Nyingma masters of the twentieth century, including Dzongsar Khyentse Chökyi Lodrö (1893–1959), Shechen Kongtrul (1901–c.

1960), and Dilgo Khyentse (1910–1991), who all considered him their root guru.

Brilliant Light by Karma Rinchen Dargye

Brilliant Light is a commentary on the practice manual of Guru Vādisiṃha as contained in the *New Treasures*. The author of the text, Karma Rinchen Dargye, states in the colophon that he intended his commentary to be a resource for practitioners of Guru Vādisiṃha, providing instructions on the practical application of the practice manual. To facilitate that, he organized the commentary according to the structure of the practice manual itself, with a few supplementary sections on specific topics, such as the particular ingredients in the offering substances, the ways to recite mantras, and the practical implementation of the unique tantric "gathering offering."

In this way, *Brilliant Light* presents the practical progression of the Vādisiṃha practice and offers supportive instructions that deepen the practitioner's understanding of the meaning behind the practices. Rinchen Dargye's style of writing is in some ways quite direct, and in other regards a clear reflection of his scholarly training, with extensive lists and descriptions that a teacher of lesser learning would be sure to avoid. While specific in form, the universality of the topic of deity practice makes *Brilliant Light* useful to anyone practicing development stage meditation, regardless of the specific nature of such practices. For those interested in the specifics of the practice itself, we have, however, at the back of the book, included a translation of the Vādisiṃha practice manual—the root text on which Rinchen Dargye bases his commentary. The practice manual was arranged by Jamgön Kongtrul based on the treasure revealed by Chokgyur Lingpa.

Rinchen Dargye, also known as Karmey Khenpo, was recognized at an early age as a reincarnated master of the Kagyu lineage whose seat was at the monastery of Karma Gön in the eastern Tibetan province of Kham. Rinchen Dargye was a close disciple of Chokgyur Lingpa himself, and he is regarded as one of the primary lineage holders of Chokgyur Lingpa's treasures. He was a prolific writer who composed a number of commentaries included in the *New Treasures*, and his own collected works constitute four volumes. His collected works are nearly all commentaries related to practices from the *New Treasures* and span an impressive variety of tantric exegesis, including two shorter works on Guru Vādisiṃha. One is a commentary on the meaning of Vādisiṃha's mantra (also included in the *New Treasures*), while the other is a brief prayer to the deities of Vādisiṃha's maṇḍala (not found in the *New Treasures*). Interestingly, the commentary on Vādisiṃha's practice manual translated here was until very recently neither contained in the *New Treasures* nor found in Rinchen Dargye's collected works.

Rinchen Dargye was an intriguing figure, who appears to have been something of an eccentric. Much of what we know about his life comes from stories in the oral tradition, passed down through masters in Chokgyur Lingpa's lineage. One unique account, which also involves Vādisiṃha, is told by Tulku Urgyen, who heard the story from a direct disciple of Rinchen Dargye (Erik Pema Kunsang and Marcia Binder Schmidt, *Blazing Splendor: The Memoirs of Tulku Urgyen Rinpoche* [Hong Kong: Rangjung Yeshe Publications, 2005], 64–65).

In Rinchen Dargye's day, each year in Lhasa all of the major monastic scholars, particularly those from the three major Gelukpa monasteries of Sera, Drepung, and Ganden, would gather to see who was the best debater. The Ganden throne holder was the judge. One year Rinchen Dargye was in Lhasa at that time and felt that he should go to join the debates. Although discouraged by his attendants, who were afraid he would lose and be embarrassed, the khenpo insisted upon participating. Having tied the wooden blocks typically used as book-covers to the front and back of his body—indicating that he himself embodied the dharma—he put his monk's shawl on over the wrong shoulder, held his rosary in the wrong hand, and put his hat flat on his head rather than standing up as it is generally worn. Thus attired, Rinchen Dargye visualized Chokgyur Lingpa at the crown of his head, visualized himself as Vādisiṃha, and set off for the debate.

Upon his turn to debate, he defeated every one of the other participants and was declared by the Ganden throne holder to be the winner. The tradition was for all participants to lay their hats on the ground and for the winner to walk over them, but Rinchen Dargye felt that to do this would be to break his vows—since part of the Buddhist refuge vows entail a commitment to respect even a shred of monastic robes—so he bowed, covered his face with his hand, and walked quietly out. Having returned to Kham, Rinchen Dargye relayed this story to Jamyang Khyentse Wangpo, who proceeded to hit Rinchen Dargye over the head with his vajra and shout at him for not walking over the opponents' hats, yelling that he could have made the Kagyu and Nyingma teachings renowned but that his attachment to his precepts had prevented that. As a practitioner of the vajra vehicle whose body is deity, voice is mantra, and mind is wisdom, he should have been able to overcome such low attachments. Rinchen Dargye is said to have quietly left his teacher's room and kept to himself for a while afterward.

Whatever the accuracy of this oral account, the story gives us a lively picture of Rinchen Dargye's great scholarship as well as his eccentric nature and his devotion to upholding his precepts. He is also said to have led a life of complete purity with respect to his monastic discipline. It seems fitting that such a learned and disciplined monk such as Rinchen Dargye should compose a commentary on the practice manual of Vādisiṃha because Vādisiṃha is portrayed in the *New Treasures* as Mañjuśrī in the form of a paṇḍita.

The Translations

These texts were translated as a project of the Dharmachakra Translation Committee under the direction of Chökyi Nyima Rinpoche. As the treasures of Chokgyur Lingpa are widely practiced in many Kagyu and Nyingma lineages, Rinpoche encouraged us to make these precious guidance texts available in English as a resource to practitioners around the world.

Divine Flower was originally translated by a group of students in a translation project class at Rangjung Yeshe Institute. The students (Zachary Beer, Anders Bjonback, Leonard Brouwer, Dorje, Michael Drews, Robin Eriksen, Rowan Fasi, Sophie Greenewalt, David Hayden, David Kesseler, Zeta Koutsokera, Franziska Oertle, Josh Schauls,

Sonam Spitz, and Alex Yiannopoulos) received oral teachings on the text, delivered directly in Tibetan by Lama Tsultrim Sangpo from Ka-Nying Shedrub Ling Monastery. During the school year, the students worked together to prepare a written draft translation. Zachary Beer later compiled these translations and then reworked them in comparison with the original Tibetan to create the final version.

Brilliant Light was translated by Catherine Dalton, originally as part of her MA thesis at the Centre for Buddhist Studies at Kathmandu University. For her translation, she also received an oral commentary on the text by Lama Tsultrim Sangpo. Catherine Dalton also translated the practice manual for Vādisiṃha that is found at the end of this book. Finally, all the manuscripts were checked against the Tibetan and edited by Andreas Doctor.

Acknowledgments

While translating these texts we have been fortunate to receive guidance and instruction from a number of learned and accomplished teachers without whose kindness the translations could not have been completed. As always, Chökyi Nyima Rinpoche continues to be a great source of guidance and inspiration and on several occasions he kindly granted the relevant empowerments and reading transmission for the practice of *Accomplishing the Guru's Mind* and Guru Vādisiṃha. We are also grateful to Tsikey Chokling Rinpoche for likewise granting empowerments for the practices of *Accomplishing the Guru's Mind* and Guru Vādisiṃha. In addition, Lama Tsultrim Sangpo offered the full reading transmission for both texts and gave a detailed oral commentary on their meaning. Additional clarifications were received from Kyabje Khenpo Tashi Palden, Tulku Jampal Dorje, Khenpo Sherab Dorje, Kunga Sangpo, and Tokpa Tulku. Finally, the translations benefited greatly from the generous advice of Erik Pema Kunsang, Marcia Schmidt, Klaus-Dieter Mathes, Douglas Duckworth, Mattia Salvini, Wiesiek Mical, Ryan Damron, and Gerry Prindiville. We also wish to thank the Tsadra Foundation for generously sponsoring the entire translation of this book.

We sincerely regret and apologize for any mistakes and errors these translations may contain. These are ours alone and stem from our limited understanding of the profound topics covered in these texts. Finally, we dedicate whatever goodness may come from this publication to the welfare and happiness of all sentient beings.

Catherine Dalton, Zachary Beer, and Andreas Doctor

Divine Flower

A Guide to the First Level of Practice of

Accomplishing the Guru's Mind: Dispeller of All Obstacles

Shechen Gyaltsap Pema Namgyal

Chokgyur Lingpa

Namo guru Vajradhārāya!
Padmasambhava—with your vajra wisdom and five spontaneously present bodies,
You are the heir of the victorious ones of the past, present, and future.
For those in need of guidance you perform a dance of myriad emanations,
And appear as our sovereign and immensely kind guru—to you I bow.

The secret and profound teachings are beyond someone like me.
Still, to fulfill the command of my peerless guru,
I respectfully offer these few notes as a divine flower.
Please keep me in your heart and grant me your blessings.

Accomplishing the Guru's Mind: Dispeller of All Obstacles contains the heart-essence of the great teacher from Uḍḍiyāṇa, the glorious one who knows the three times. It is therefore the foremost treasure among all those that were buried in the land of Tibet. The instructions on its first level of practice can be summarized in three parts:

1. The preliminary trainings
2. The main practice
3. The conclusion

The Preliminary Trainings

The preliminary trainings consist of (1) the general preliminaries, (2) generating renunciation, and (3) the unique preliminaries that plant the seeds.

The General Preliminaries

The general preliminaries are further divided into (1) the preliminaries for a session and (2) the preliminaries of instruction.

Preliminaries for a Session

Sit in meditation posture in a secluded place and clear your stale breath. Visualize your guru above your head and then, with the devotion of seeing him as a buddha in person, supplicate him by saying: "Essence of all the buddhas of the three times, precious guru, please think of me and bless my mind-stream." Then, imagine that the guru melts into light and dissolves into you. At that point you should settle in the unfabricated natural state for as long as it lasts. This is a way for extraordinary blessings to arise in one's mind-stream, so from now on, practice it at the beginning of every session.

Preliminaries of Instruction

The root text says:

> The one who has attained the supreme freedoms and
> advantages
> And is weary of impermanence
> Should strive, with deep renunciation,
> To discriminate according to cause and effect.
> That fortunate one who has trust and compassion . . .

Accordingly, these instructions have four sections: (1) the difficulty of obtaining the freedoms and advantages, (2) the impermanence of life, (3) the flaws of cyclic existence, and (4) the cause and effect of actions.

The Difficulty of Obtaining the Freedoms and Advantages

This section is divided into (1) identifying the freedoms and advantages, (2) understanding how difficult they are to attain, and (3) reflecting on the great value of what has been attained.

Identifying the Freedoms and Advantages

Now that we have attained the precious human body with the eighteen freedoms and advantages, the perfect support for enlightenment, we should strive to take advantage of it as best we can. The eight freedoms are mentioned in *The Great Commentary on the Perfection of Wisdom in Eight Thousand Verses*, which says:

> Hell beings, hungry spirits, animals, barbarians, long-lived gods, those with wrong views, living in a time without a buddha, having impaired faculties: these are the eight states in which one is not free.

Those who are born in the three lower realms suffer intensely and have an inferior bodily support, and so lack the freedom to practice the Dharma. The long-lived gods lack the perception required for learning and reflection, while other gods are attached to sense pleasures or intoxicated in a state of absorption, and so they are also not free to practice the Dharma. These are the four nonhuman states that are not free.

Even those born as a human may be born in a realm with no buddha. They may also be born where there is a buddha, but as a barbarian in a borderland where the Dharma has not spread. They may be born in a place where the Dharma has spread, but have the wrong view of not believing in the Three Jewels, the cause and effect of actions, and past and future lives. They may be mute and dumb, and thus not be able to understand what they should and should not do. To "have freedom" means to be free from these eight—including these four human states. About this, *The Dharma Compendium Sūtra* says: "Escaping from the eight unfree states, you are always at leisure."

Among the ten advantages, first there are five personal advantages:

> Born human, in a central place, with all one's faculties,
> Without a conflicting lifestyle, and with faith in the Dharma.

In general we have attained a human body and in particular we have been born in a central place where the Dharma has spread. Because our five sense faculties are intact, we are capable of knowing what we should and should not do. So far in this life we have not committed deeds such as those with immediate retribution, and so we are capable of following the path. We have trust in the true Dharma taught by the Buddha, such as the *vinaya*. These five are called the personal advantages because they are present in one's own being, and they are conditions for practicing the Dharma.

The five advantages that come from others are:

> A buddha has appeared and has taught the Dharma.
> The teachings still remain and they are followed.
> There are those who are kind toward others.

The Buddha appeared in the world, and he taught the true Dharma. Those teachings have remained without diminishing, and there are still many people who follow the teachings. There are people who out of their kindness support Dharma practitioners, and in particular there are spiritual teachers who compassionately take on students. These are called the five advantages from others because they are embodied in others and are conditions for practicing the Dharma. In this way, the freedoms are the essence of the precious human body, while the advantages are its distinctive features.

To practice this, think to yourself: "Now this one time, I have attained a body complete with the eighteen freedoms and advantages; I must persevere in the true Dharma. If I don't, how much more could I betray myself?" *The Way of the Bodhisattva* also speaks of this:

> Now that I have gained such freedoms as these,
> If I still do not train myself in virtue,
> How much more could I betray myself?
> There could never be anything more foolish.

The Difficulty of Attaining the Freedoms and Advantages

It is said that among sentient beings, those in the lower realms are limitless, numerous as the dust particles in the whole world, while those in the higher realms are extremely few, like the dust particles on a fingernail. Out of the three lower realms, there is the smallest number of animals. Among them, the vast majority live underwater, in the great oceans and so on, while a smaller number live dispersed among the realms of gods and men. Even compared to these, however, the number of human beings is generally very small, and the number of humans on Jambudvīpa is especially few. On top of all this, to attain a human body with a connection to the Dharma is next to impossible.

The reason for this scarcity is that there are so many sentient beings who engage in harmful deeds, while only a few are engaged in positive ones. Moreover, among those doing positive things it is very rare to find anyone who also lives a life of discipline, which creates a momentum toward the higher realms. Furthermore, having the right aspiration at the time of death is very important as a condition for taking a good rebirth, yet this is also rare. Therefore, since it is rare that such causes and conditions are gathered, this precious human body is very difficult to attain. An analogy of this is given in *Letter to a Friend*:

> It is much easier for a turtle to surface by chance
> Through a ring on the ocean than it is for an animal
> To be reborn as a human. So practice the true Dharma,
> Your Majesty, and enjoy the happiness that it brings.

In particular, to attain a human body with a real connection to the Dharma, first one must have a wish to practice the true Dharma, and then one should use that wish to accumulate great amounts of merit through acts such as generosity. So therefore, think to yourself, "Now that I have attained a body that is so difficult to attain, and a mind that is such a perfect support, I will by all means practice the genuine Dharma in order to achieve lasting happiness."

The Great Value of the Precious Human Body

With this perfect support one can easily accomplish all the temporary enjoyments of the higher realms, which is where the path of lesser beings leads. However, one can also achieve the state of passing beyond suffering according to the lower vehicle, which is the path of middling beings. Finally, it is even possible to reach enlightenment, which is the unsurpassable path that great beings traverse. On the other hand, without a physical support like this, there is no way to achieve even worldly happiness, let alone liberation. So now, motivate yourself from the bottom of your heart with a commitment to make full use of these freedoms and advantages! *The Way of the Bodhisattva* speaks of this:

> Use this boat of a human body
> To cross the wide river of suffering.
> Such a boat will later be hard to find,
> So don't go back to sleep now, you fool!

Impermanence and Death

This section is divided into three discussions of (1) the certainty of death, (2) the unpredictability of the time of death, and (3) the fact that at the moment of death nothing will be of benefit.

The Certainty of Death

We all know that we are going to die at some point. Still, until the very moment comes, we cling to a foolish expectation that it will not happen right away. Deceiving ourselves in this way, we remain lost in this life's distractions, lazily putting off the pursuit of any aim of lasting importance. To remedy this it is important to contemplate impermanence. No matter the birth we have taken, or the friends we rely on, we are not going to escape death. In the past there has never been anyone who did not die, and neither will there ever be such a person. In particular, we have seen directly so many friends, enemies, and strangers die, so why do we feel so sure that we ourselves will not? It says in a sūtra:

> All who ever lived and all those to come
> Must pass away, leaving their body behind.
> The wise understand that all will perish,
> So rely on the Dharma and put it to practice!

Not only are we not beyond death, but in fact we are approaching it with every passing year, month, day, hour, and moment. The time spent can never come back; our life continuously dwindles away. It says in *The Way of the Bodhisattva*:

> Never pausing, both day and night,
> This life is constantly slipping away.
> That which has passed will never return,
> So how could someone like me escape death?

Early on, when we are young, we lack the will to pursue the Dharma. Later, when we are old, we may act like we are practicing the Dharma, but our physical and mental vigor is spent, so we do not make any progress. In between, half of our time is spent asleep, while the other half is spent entirely on meaningless things like wandering around, hanging out, doing this and that, while time presses on. Consider how this leaves not the slightest chance to practice, and apply yourself diligently to the Dharma.

The Unpredictability of the Time of Death

Except for those who live on the continent of Unpleasant Sound, sentient beings do not have a fixed life span. However, particularly uncertain is the life span of those who live on Jambudvīpa, especially in these times when the five degenerations are rampant. As such, there are treasure prophecies predicting that, in the future, people will have a lifespan of only thirty years. Still, even though it may currently be possible for people to reach sixty or seventy years by the force of their previous good deeds, the counting process has long since begun! What has passed is already gone; what remains we cannot say for sure. No one can say for sure whether we will die old, young, or middle-aged. Just consider how often we witness or hear of people suddenly dying—that could just as well happen to us. Since we honestly don't know which will come earlier—tomorrow or the next life—what is the point of getting so caught up in this life's activities?

The body is as fragile as a bubble on the water. Our breath, like mist, is ready to fade away. Unless we gain control of our minds, there is no certainty where we will end up. There are so many ways to die, and even our attempts at staying alive may often become a cause of death. That is why we should contemplate the fact that the time of our death is as unpredictable as a candle in the wind. As it is said in *The Way of a Bodhisattva*:

> To think, "At least today I will not die,"
> And take comfort in that is senseless.

Nāgārjuna also says:

There are so many ways to die,
And so few ways to stay alive,
And even they can lead to death,
So practice the Dharma constantly!

At Death Only the Dharma Will Be of Benefit

When death suddenly arrives, all the wealth we have accumulated will not be of any help since we cannot bring it with us. Our friends and relatives who have kept us company will also not be of benefit since they cannot guide us along. Likewise, the house that we built will be useless and unable to shelter us any more. Even the very flesh and bones we were born with will be left behind, while we must wander aimlessly through the intermediate state all by ourselves. All that comes along with us are the actions, wholesome or unwholesome, that we have gathered. It says in *The Sūtra of Advice to the King*:

Your Majesty, time is running out and when you pass away,
Your wealth, friends, relatives, and loved ones do not follow.
Wherever beings come from and wherever they may go,
All that follows after them is their karma, like a shadow.

When we understand that all the changes that the universe and its inhabitants undergo are signs that demonstrate impermanence to us, we will come to see how this life's activities are never-ending and futile. At that point, we must make a resolution to do nothing besides practice the genuine Dharma since only that will help us at the time of death and beyond. With that resolute commitment, apply yourself to the Dharma without wasting time, like a beautiful girl whose hair has caught fire. It says in *Letter to a Friend*:

If suddenly your hair or clothes caught on fire,
You would drop what you were doing to put it out.
Make the same effort to not be reborn—
There is nothing of greater importance than that!

As the Omniscient Lord of Dharma said:

> This life is as transient as a vase made of clay.
> Tomorrow's experience or that of the next life—
> Which will come first, there is no guarantee,
> So practice the true Dharma starting today.

The Flaws of Cyclic Existence

The flaws of cyclic existence are explained in terms of (1) the suffering of the lower realms, (2) the suffering of the higher realms, and (3) general reflections on the three types of suffering.

The Suffering of the Lower Realms

Not only will our death be out of our control, we also have to take rebirth. Since we have not yet transcended the higher and lower realms of saṃsāra, our positive or negative karma will propel us helplessly right back into them. Just think of how many negative and harmful deeds we have accumulated in this life alone. Beyond this, many more habits created in previous lives and subsequently stored in the all-ground are yet to ripen. So why are we so confident that we will not be born in the lower realms? Instead, wouldn't it be better to consider the different types of suffering that will await us if we are born there? Nāgārjuna has said:

> Imagine one day as a hell being
> In the extremes of heat or cold.
> Or consider the hungry spirits,
> Emaciated by hunger and thirst.
> Look around and reflect on the anguish
> Of the animals in utter delusion.
> Then abandon the causes of these states,
> And create the causes for happiness.

The Suffering in the Hells

The Hot Hells

The hot hell realms are filled with mountains, canyons, and rocky landscapes and a ground of burning iron. Flames as high as a cubit blaze continuously, while molten copper and acid rain down. They are filled with blazing trees of burning iron, and replete with all sorts of wild and vicious birds, beasts, and the henchmen of Yama, guardians of hell. Walls of burning iron and fire pits surround them. It is said that they are hotter than the fires during an eon's age of destruction, and that the heat multiplies four times with each lower realm. The beings in the intermediate state who are to be born there feel cold and as if they were being swept away by a tempest. Seeing the hot hells and recognizing their warmth, they hurry there in longing for it. The moment they enter, they take birth there, as if awaking from sleep. They have bodies that are soft, tender, and sensitive, so they cannot bear much either physically or mentally; thus their agony is especially great.

The Various Hot Hells

The beings in the Hell of Revival perceive each other as enemies, becoming fiercely enraged. By the power of their karma, various weapons appear in their hands, and they strike each other until, in intense agony, they collapse and lose consciousness. Then they are revived, either by a voice from the sky, calling out "Revive!" or by cold winds that stir up, and so they go through the same unbearable pain as before until their karma is exhausted.

The beings in the Black Line Hell have four, eight, or more black lines drawn on their bodies by the guardians of hell. Then they suffer through being cut and chopped along the lines by saws, axes, and the like.

The beings in the Hell of Crushing suffer by having their bodies inserted and then pressed between iron mountains shaped like the heads of goats, rams, tigers, lions, and the like. They are ground like sesame seeds in giant iron mortars and pounded by a rainfall of burning iron boulders until they are crushed into powder.

The beings in the Hell of Howling, searching in panic for a safe haven, come across an iron building. When they enter into it, the door immediately shuts and fires blaze up everywhere, inside and out. Thus they suffer, wailing and calling out in despair, but finding no refuge.

The beings in the Hell of Great Howling suffer even more intensely: here they are burned in a double-walled iron building.

The beings in the Hell of Heat are burned by blazing fires inside iron cauldrons several leagues in size. They are impaled through the anus straight up to the crown of their head by flaming iron stakes. Thus they suffer through being entirely roasted, even down to their internal organs.

The beings in the Hell of Intense Heat suffer by having their bodies impaled by tridents through their anus, up and out of their head and two shoulders. They are wrapped up in flaming iron blankets and cooked upside down in acid in iron cauldrons.

The beings in the Hell of Ultimate Torment have the flesh of their bodies scorched down to the marrow of their bones by a ground of burning iron that blazes up in every direction. They themselves blaze in a way that is indistinguishable from the flames, so that only by the moans they let out are they revealed as sentient beings. They are also roasted in burning embers mixed with iron filings. They are made to repeatedly climb up and down huge mountains of burning iron. They have their tongues stretched out on a ground of burning iron and then stabbed by daggers. Their skin is peeled off. Their jaws are pried wide open, and then they are made to swallow lumps of iron and molten copper, burning their mouth, throat, and all their internal organs. There could be no worse torment than the unbearable agony these beings must go through; thus it is called Ultimate Torment.

About their specific life spans, it says in *The Treasury of Abhidharma*:

> A day in the first six, such as Reviving,
> Is equal to the lifetime of a god in the desire realm.

One day in the heavens of the four great kings is equal to fifty human years and the beings there can live up to fifty of their own years. This, added up, makes one day for beings in the Hell of Reviving, and their life span is five hundred of their own years. The life span doubles with each lower hell, while the number of days in a year also doubles. Thus, the life span in each of the lower hells is four times that of the one above it. It is said that one remains in the Hell of Intense Heat for half an intermediate eon, and for one intermediate eon in the Hell of Ultimate Torment.

The Cold Hells

These realms are engulfed in darkness, as there is no sun or moon. There are gorges covered in ice and snow, engulfed by freezing blizzards and windstorms. Each level lower is said to be seven times colder than the previous. Beings in the intermediate state who are to take birth there feel as if they are being burned by fire. Seeing the cold hells, they long for them, and, hurrying toward them, they take birth there.

The Various Cold Hells

Beings in the Hell of Blisters suffer in freezing windstorms and blizzards, which cause them to curl up while blisters suddenly break out all over their bodies.

Beings in the Hell of Burst Blisters suffer furthermore through having their blisters burst open by the freezing cold. Metal parasites hatch inside them and rip their flesh apart. The blood and lymph then runs out and freezes solid.

Beings in the Hell of Whimpering moan in despair. With their faint voices they can only utter mere noises.

It is even colder in the Hell of Lamentations, where beings cannot even make comprehensible sounds, but only faint moans of pain.

Yet in the Hell of Chattering Teeth it is so much colder that beings there cannot use their voices at all. Their bodies tremble in agony, and their teeth chatter.

In the Hell of Blue Lotus-like Cracks, the force of the cold, which is still more intense, causes beings' skin to turn blue and burst open into cracks of five or six pieces.

In the Hell of Red Lotus-like Cracks, their skin passes beyond blue until it becomes red in color, cracking open into ten or even more pieces.

In the Hell of the Great Lotus-like Cracks, beings suffer unbearably through the most extreme cold. Their skin peels off, cracking open into hundreds or thousands of pieces, leaving them utterly red and raw.

About their specific life spans, it is says in *The Treasury of Abhidharma*:

> The length of time it takes to empty a bin of sesame,
> By removing just one seed every hundred years,
> Is equal to the life span in the Hell of Blisters.
> For the life span of the others, this is multiplied by twenty.

Here a "bin of sesame" means a container which could fit eighty Magadha units, filled to the brim with sesame seeds. The amount of time it would take, removing one seed every hundred years, to empty all the sesame seeds equals the life span in the Hell of Blisters. It is explained that this life span is prolonged twenty times for each lower realm.

The Neighboring Hells

In each of the four cardinal directions of the hot hells are four neighboring hells, such as the pit of hot embers, making sixteen altogether. Beings end up there either by escaping the hot hells or by directly taking birth there. Once here, they try to flee but only end up in a pit of blazing embers. With every step they take in this pit, their skin and flesh are instantly roasted, only to heal as they lift their foot again. Even if they escape, they fall into a reeking swamp of rotting corpses, where parasites with sharp mandibles feed on them, burrowing into their skin and flesh, right down to the bones.

If they are somehow able to get free from that, they arrive on a plain filled with razors where their feet are constantly ripped to shreds and then healed again. At the end of this plain, they arrive at a forest of swords. They sit down to rest in the shade of the trees, but suddenly their karmic wind picks up and swords pour down from above, slicing them to pieces. When they then collapse, dogs gather and devour them. After that they are suddenly revived and, seeing a forest of iron thorn trees, they hurry toward it. But the trees have sharp thorns sixteen inches long that point down when the beings climb up them and upward when they climb down. The thorns puncture their bodies like a sieve, and then ravens and other birds with iron beaks peck out their eyeballs and flesh.

The beings in these neighboring hells undergo so much suffering, but should any of them escape, their torment continues as they now find themselves overwhelmed by extreme heat. In the distance they then see a cascading river and rush toward it, but fall into what is actually a stream of burning-hot acid. Sinking to the bottom, their flesh dislodges from their bones. Rising to the surface, they are reborn and begin to sink again. Though they long to escape, fierce hell guardians stand guard on both banks, and don't allow them to. Thus they suffer in so many ways.

Considering the plain of razor blades, the forest of swords, and the forest of iron thorn trees as one, there are four neighboring hells. Though there is no explanation of a set life span among these, one must remain in each for hundreds, or even thousands of years.

The Ephemeral Hells

There are also hells known as the ephemeral hells. They are found in a variety of places, from the periphery of the main hell realms to ocean shores, both underground and above. Their particular forms of suffering include being burned by fire, being frozen and split open, and getting killed by slaughterers and then eaten. The experience of beings in these hells is never predictable, and they constantly switch back and forth between feeling pleasure and pain. This is mentioned in *Letter to a Friend*, which says:

> Imagine the pain of three hundred spears
> Piercing your body at full force for an entire day.
> That does not compare, even in the slightest,
> To a fraction of the pain in the hells.

The reasons for ending up in such suffering are entirely one's own unwholesome actions, such as killing, so we should take care to avoid such conduct.

The Suffering of the Hungry Spirits

The hungry spirits for the most part live five hundred leagues below this world, but some also live aboveground, scattered throughout the landscape. *The Application of Mindfulness* describes them as being of thirty-six types, but these can be summed up in the following three.

Externally obscured hungry spirits are tormented by hunger and thirst, have dry mouths and emaciated bodies. Their necks and limbs are thin, and their hair is tangled. Though they are constantly rushing around in search of food and drink, they don't find any. From a distance they might see things such as food, streams, and fruit trees, but when they approach, there is usually not the slightest trace of them, and instead only pus, blood, and coal. In other cases what they see may not transform in such a way, but is nonetheless guarded by beings armed with weapons, and so they are not able to enjoy them.

Internally obscured hungry spirits have mouths as small a needle's eye and throats as thin as a hair from a horse's tail, yet their stomachs are as big as a great valley. They never have anything to eat or drink, and even if they do find a little, they cannot fit it in their mouths. Even should they manage to stuff some food in their mouths, it ends up disappearing in their throat. Moreover, a poison in their mouth dries up any drink they may take, so that even if they swallow a little bit, it does not go down their throat. Even so, should any food or liquid nevertheless happen to enter their belly, it will never satisfy their hunger.

Hungry spirits with specific obscurations suffer because they have to eat food that later becomes disgusting and painful. When they take food and drink, it catches fire and burns their intestines and other organs. Otherwise their food turns into poison and fire, or filthy, foul-smelling things like excrement, urine, pus, and blood.

In this way, all types of hungry spirits suffer constantly from hunger and thirst. Moreover, they have no clothes, and so during summertime even the moon scorches them, while in the winter even the rays of the sun feel cold. They also become weary and fatigued by their constant searching. Since their bodies are feeble, their joints get dislocated and catch fire. Moreover, they become mutual enemies and bind and beat each other. In this way, they live in great fear of being killed because they have no safe haven. In these and other ways, they have to experience intense, prolonged suffering.

Regarding their life span, *The Treasury of Abhidharma* says that one month for them is five hundred days. *Letter to a Friend* says that, "they will not die for five and ten thousand years." This is so because one day for them is one human month and they live for five hundred of their own years, which equals fifteen thousand human years. The cause for this type of suffering is miserliness, which includes acts such as preventing others from giving. Therefore, we must refrain from this type of conduct and carefully watch our actions.

The Suffering of Animals

Some animals live underwater in the great oceans. Without a home or any protection, and tossed about by the waves, they roam around at random. They feed on each other, the large ones swallowing the small ones whole, the smaller ones boring into the larger ones' bodies. Nāgas suffer unbearably from being scorched every day by hot sand, and in the constant fear of being eaten by their predators such as garudas.

Others live scattered among the realms of gods and humans. Wild animals have no ease of mind because they are constantly tormented by the fear of their predators. They are devoured by birds and carnivorous animals or killed helplessly by humans. Those domesticated by humans have their fur sheared off and their noses pierced. They are beaten, prodded, and tormented with heavy loads. They are killed for their meat, blood, skin, and bones. Thus they suffer, dumb and dull, living in a stupor with no comprehension of what to do and what not to do. They also suffer in other visible ways that are similar to hell beings and hungry spirits, such as by hunger, thirst, heat, cold, and exhaustion. It is said, "the life-span of animals is a supremely long eon," meaning for those that live the longest, it may be about an eon, while for the shortest it is uncertain.

This is how to reflect on the suffering of the lower realms. Right now, it is difficult for us merely to put a finger into a flame for a short moment, stay naked in ice in the dead of winter, spend a whole day without food and drink, be stung by bees, or bitten by fleas. So how could we handle the suffering in the three lower realms? Relate it to your own present experience, and use the dread that comes from this to inspire yourself with heartfelt disillusionment and renunciation and make full use of your freedoms and advantages.

The Flaws of the Higher Realms

The accumulation of positive deeds corresponding to merit on the lesser, middle, and greater paths results in taking birth respectively as a human, a god in the desire realm, and a god in the upper realms. Once there, one enjoys the resulting temporary happiness, but it is transitory and impermanent. Therefore all the realms of cyclic existence, whether high or low, are not beyond the nature of suffering.

This section is divided into (1) the suffering of humans, (2) the suffering of demigods, and (3) the suffering of gods.

The Suffering of Humans

In general, the sufferings of birth, old age, sickness, and death are immeasurable. Before we are born, we have to spend many months in our mother's womb, which is an unbearably cramped, dark, and foul-smelling place with fluctuating temperature. Then, when it comes time to be born, we suffer as our body is flipped upside down and squeezed out, as through the hole in a draw-plate. Just out of the womb, when people touch us, it feels like being whipped by thorns. When we are picked up, we feel like a baby bird being snatched off by a hawk.

Later in life, we eventually become old, and our complexion fades, turning to an unpleasant ashy color. Our hair turns white, and our senses become dull. Our physique deteriorates, and our teeth fall out. The body becomes hunched over and the limbs crooked and thin. The skin turns slack and the face wrinkled. Our strength weakens so that we can hardly stand up. Instead of walking, we hobble along, and when sitting, we slump over. Our speech becomes gibberish. The senses weaken so that the vision becomes blurry and the ears go deaf. Our wealth may diminish so that we lack food and have to go hungry. Even if we have enough, it is hard to enjoy good things because of digestion problems and the like. Everything irritates us, and when we are stricken with illness due to various circumstances and previous actions, it feels overwhelmingly painful as our body deteriorates. We lose the ability to enjoy otherwise pleasurable things such as food, drink, and sleep. Instead, we are forced to submit to harsh medicines, and procedures such as bloodletting and moxibustion.

The fear of death also creates limitless suffering. When it is time to die, even medical treatment and rituals are of no benefit. Thus, everything we worked so hard to acquire—our wealth, power, friends and companions, even our dear and cherished body—must be left behind. There is intense pain as the life force is cut; then we die and begin to wander helplessly in the intermediate state.

In the brief interval between these four particular types of suffering, we readily endure any risk to life and limb just to achieve the mundane comforts that wealth and influence may bring. Even so, we also undergo the suffering of not getting what we want as well as the suffering of meeting, or fearing to meet, unpleasant things such as intense heat, cold, hunger, thirst, illness, evil spirits, enemies, and bandits. We also suffer when we must part from those joys and pleasures that we love and cherish, including the happiness that our friends, family, and enjoyments bring us.

In short, once the defiled aggregates have formed, suffering is unavoidable. If we are wealthy, the more staff and wealth we have, the more we worry about keeping it all. Yet if we are poor, we may work hard but still not have sufficient food, clothing, and other such necessities. *The Succession of Lives* mentions this:

> One is in distress to keep what he has,
> Another is exhausted by searching.
> One may be rich, one may be poor,
> But neither finds happiness anywhere.

This simply points out what we can see firsthand.

The Suffering of the Demigods

Seeing the splendors of the gods, the demigods are struck with an overwhelming envy, which for them is a result similar to its cause. Because of it, they continuously start fights with the gods, but they have less merit, and so they wind up in immense pain—being beaten, having their limbs chopped or torn off, and even being killed. The gods survive even if struck in a vital point, unless they are decapitated or cut in half at the waist. Demigods, however, are similar to humans, and so when they are struck in a vital point, they die. Their reflection then appears in the surface of a lake known as "Radiance," which is located at the golden basis of the world. Seeing this, their friends and relatives are stricken with sorrow even before the other combatants return from battle. Most demigods are evil beings who despise the Dharma. A few of them, however, may develop an interest, but they are so obscured that they are unable to reach any special realization.

The Suffering of the Gods

The suffering of the gods is described in terms of those who live in the desire realm and those who live in the upper god realms.

Gods in the desire realm are so distracted by their pleasures that they do not notice that their life is slipping away. Then, seven god realm days before their death, five omens of death appear. Their complexion becomes unpleasant, and they feel uncomfortable sitting on their throne. Their flower garland wilts, and their garments start to smell bad. Finally, their bodies start to sweat, something that never happened to them before. Thus they suffer through an arduous and drawn-out dying process. Their divine partners and their retinue abandon them and move on to other gods, which only further aggravates their pain and depression.

Moreover, although they are so deeply attached to their divine riches, they know they must leave them all behind. They are also aware that in their next life it will be almost impossible to be reborn again as a god, that it is unlikely that they will be reborn as a human, and that probably they will take birth in the lower realms, where they will have to experience agonizing and prolonged misery. This knowledge creates overwhelming suffering. *The Sūtra of the Application of Mindfulness* describes this:

> The agony of falling
> From the abode of the gods
> Is much more intense
> Than the sufferings of hell.

Furthermore, by seeing gods of greater merit, those of lesser merit become dejected, and those of greater power expel the weaker gods from their abodes. In particular, the gods in the heaven of the four great kings and the abode of the thirty-three fight and clash with the demigods, who wound them with their weapons and occasionally even kill them. In so many ways they experience intense suffering.

The gods in the form and formless realms do not experience any noticeable form of suffering, yet, since they are still subject to conditioned existence, they do have to face this basic form of suffering. Intoxicated by a state of meditative absorption, these gods do not strive to improve themselves. They cannot bear to lose the flavor of their absorption, and when they eventually do lose that state, they die. Moreover, when the momentum of the previous actions that caused them to dwell in these realms is exhausted, they once again take rebirth in the desire realm, especially its lower realms. This is described in *Letter to a Friend*:

> Having lived among the lavish pleasures of the desire gods,
> And the detached bliss of the Brahma states,
> Once again they must face incessant pain
> As fuel for the flames of ultimate torment.

Therefore, wherever we are born in the three realms, whether in the higher or lower states of cyclic existence, we are never beyond suffering. Wherever we live, whomever we befriend, whatever we enjoy, it will all be unsatisfying. *The Supreme Continuum* speaks of this:

> Just as excrement never smells good,
> The five types of beings will never be happy.
> Their suffering is like constant contact
> With fire, weapons, and acid.

The Three Types of Suffering

In general, wherever we are born in cyclic existence, whether high or low, we experience nothing but the causes and effects of suffering. Some, as a result of minor generosity in past lives and the momentum it has created, are born as a human or a god. Although they may superficially enjoy many servants and pleasures, they often do so with a negative attitude. This leads them to engage in lots of harmful behavior, which in turn creates the causes for later experiencing the inescapable sufferings of hell as well as the other lower realms. Thus they must endure the many overwhelming and prolonged types of suffering that are found in the three lower realms and elsewhere. These sufferings can all be summed up in the following three types.

The suffering of suffering means that one suffers as soon as one is born. For such a being, everything is unpleasant, threatening, and feels painful, whether due to intense heat, cold, hunger, or thirst. This type of suffering is primarily experienced in the three lower realms.

The suffering of change refers to the fact that everything in the desire realm is impermanent and subject to change, whether it be one's long life, possessions, or the tainted meditation states. This also includes all types of pleasures since their impermanence causes suffering. This type of suffering is primarily experienced by humans and gods in the desire realm.

The all-pervasive suffering of conditioned existence is the basis for both of the above types of suffering. It refers to the mere assembly of the perpetuating aggregates, which function as the source of all types of suffering. In this way, it is the matrix out of which all painful states, such as birth and old age, gradually develop. Therefore, the state of feeling mere indifference is termed the "pervasive suffering of conditioned existence." This refers mainly to the four absorptions and the four formless realms. This is also mentioned in a sūtra that says:

> No matter what kinds of feeling you may have, they are all suffering.

We must understand that unless we free ourselves from the suffering of conditioned existence, there is no way to avoid the suffering of suffering and the suffering of change, just as a tree is not felled by chopping its branches without cutting the root.

The Cause and Effect of Actions

This section consists of (1) a general reflection on actions and their effects, (2) a reflection on specific instances, and (3) a concluding summary regarding the four truths based on a subsidiary reflection on the nature of trust.

A General Reflection

Generally speaking, wholesome actions lead to happiness whether they are positive attitudes or helpful deeds. On the other hand, unwholesome actions, such as attitudes involving the three poisons and harmful physical deeds, result in suffering. The Buddha himself described the inconceivable ways that positive and negative actions ripen without fail into specific results, so now we must discriminate accordingly. An action, whether wholesome or harmful, may seem small when it is done, while still a cause. When it ripens into a result, however, it may have multiplied a hundred or a thousand times. In some cases it may even be that it multiplies in a way that is beyond measure, just as barley and other plants grow and multiply from a single seed. Unless an opposing force overcomes our accumulated actions, they cannot possibly dissipate before their results have ripened. For this reason, it is important to take heed of the key points of what to do and what to avoid. As it says in a sūtra:

> The actions of beings are not erased
> Even over one hundred eons,
> For when the time comes and conditions gather,
> They will ripen into results.

Reflecting on Specific Instances

This section contains reflections on (1) the unwholesome deeds that should be avoided, (2) the wholesome deeds that should be performed, and (3) the way to transform neutral deeds into wholesome actions.

The Unwholesome Deeds

As described above, there are deeds that are inherently wrong. Whether in thought or behavior, they are negative no matter who carries them out. There are also deeds that are said to be "wrong by violation," which refers to actions through which a person breaks his or her vows. These two types of unwholesome deeds are in fact the cause of all the suffering in cyclic existence. Although there are lengthy enumerations of them, the main points about which deeds we should adopt and avoid can be condensed into the following list of ten.

First, there are three physical misdeeds.

1. Taking life means to kill without mistaking the victim, with the intent to do so, and without changing one's mind until the other being is dead.

2. To take what is not given refers to stealing or robbing someone else's possessions that are not being freely given, and with the wish to acquire them for oneself.

3. Sexual misconduct can refer to having an inappropriate partner, such as someone else's wife, a relative within seven or eight degrees of kinship, a prostitute working for a fee, someone in the custody of others—whether their parents or a king, or someone who is upholding a vow of celibacy. It can also refer to an inappropriate occasion, such as when one's partner is ill, in distress, pregnant, menstruating, or if indulged in constantly. Sexual misconduct can also be due to an inappropriate location, such as having sexual relations at a stūpa or a temple, near a congregation of nuns, or on a hard or bumpy surface that may injure one's partner. Finally, it can refer to having sexual activity in an improper pathway, meaning any orifice other than the genitals. All of the above behavior concerns laypeople, while for those upholding celibacy, sexual misconduct would be any type of unchaste behavior.

Secondly, there are four verbal misdeeds.

4. Lying is to deliberately say something untrue (thus distorting a fact with the intention to deceive) to another person who actually hears what is being said. This is not limited to verbal communication since it can also be done with physical gestures.

5. Divisive speech refers to the use of disturbing words that are understood by the people they are spoken to with the wish to cause friction among people who are otherwise getting along.

6. Harsh speech means to say things that hurt the feelings of others who are present, such as describing their faults. This must be understood by the people it is spoken to.

7. Idle chatter refers to speech that is not one of the three above-mentioned types. It includes flattery, singing, and dramatic performance, as well as discussion of war, business dealings, or lust. It also includes the religious discourses of those with wrong views.

Finally, there are three mental misdeeds.

8. Covetousness means to have a deep wish to own someone else's things, such as their home, possessions, friends, or servants.

9. Ill will means to have a strong wish to harm someone, thus hoping that they will suffer.

10. Wrong view means to hold narrow-minded beliefs, such as thinking that actions do not truly have results, that the Three Jewels do not exist, or that there are no past and future lives.

This list of misdeeds describes acts that have been fully completed. We should, however, also take care to discipline ourselves so that we avoid any resembling actions, such as killing beings unintentionally or by accident.

These unwholesome deeds lead to three types of effect: the ripened effect, the correlated effect, and the dominant effect.

The ripened effect can itself be of three types—greater, medium, or lesser—depending on the strength of one's intention. The greater type leads to rebirth as a hell being, the medium to rebirth as a hungry spirit, and the lesser to rebirth as an animal. Born in these lower realms, one goes through the various painful experiences described above.

The correlated effect first involves an experience similar to the cause. Killing, for instance, leads to a short life, stealing to poverty, and sexual misconduct to an abundance of enemies. Lying leads to being slandered, divisive speech to being resented by friends, harsh speech to hearing unpleasant words, and idle chatter to people disregarding your word. Covetousness leads to unfulfilled hopes, ill will to a life in fear, and wrong view to stupidity and delusion. The correlated effect also entails a behavior similar to the cause, which means that in the future one will continue to enjoy the same actions that one performed in the past.

The dominant effect refers to a karmic ripening in the outer environment. Taking life leads to grains and medicinal plants lacking potency, stealing to poor harvests, and sexual misconduct to an environment that is filled with dust, haze, and mist. Lying leads to an environment that is filthy and foul smelling, divisive speech to an uneven landscape with cliffs and chasms, harsh speech to arid plains full of salt and thorn bushes, and idle chatter to imbalances in the passing of the four seasons. Covetousness leads to poor and meager crops, ill will to spoiled crops that would otherwise be tasty and nutritious, and wrong view to crops diminishing until they finally vanish altogether.

The correlated and the dominant effects can manifest at any time, whether in the present life or a future one.

The Wholesome Deeds

In general, there are countless wholesome deeds that those in need of training can perform to remedy the eighty-four thousand disturbing emotions that should be removed from their minds. However, these are all in effect included if we simply resolve to give up the ten unwholesome deeds and then keep a strong commitment to avoid any further unwholesome acts, whether physical or verbal.

"Resolving to give up the ten unwholesome deeds" means to recognize that unwholesome deeds are negative after seeing their flaws and then to avoid them at all times. "To avoid any further unwholesome acts, whether physical or verbal" means that after forming this resolve and staying mindful of it, we do not carry out negative deeds, even when at times a seemingly profitable situation would have otherwise led us carelessly to do so. For the seven physical and verbal deeds, it is necessary both to make the resolve and stay mindful. For the three that are mental, however, the resolve alone suffices. This type of determination serves not only as a remedy to unwholesome deeds, but also as the core of the discipline of precepts. It is said:

> The resolve to give up unwholesome deeds
> Is taught as the perfection of discipline.

Whenever we are strongly committed to refraining from unwholesome deeds, obstacles like drowsiness, dullness, and distraction may occur. However, if we notice these states and see them to be flawed, we can stop them. This ability comes from the strength of that previous momentum, which is like a seed. In this way, the commitment to relinquish the ten unwholesome deeds, along with the potential this commitment creates, constitutes in itself the ten wholesome deeds. However, in terms of building positive qualities, we should always strive to act, speak, and think in wholesome ways by engaging in the ten harmonious acts, such as protecting life, as well as the ten Dharma activities.

The effects of the ten wholesome deeds are also discussed in terms of the ripened effect, the correlated effect, and the dominant effect.

The ripened effect manifests in three degrees of goodness—greater, medium, and lesser—depending on whether the wholesome deed was carried out from beginning to end with a positive mind-set or not. The greater degree leads to birth as a god in the upper realms, the medium to birth as a god in the desire realm, and the lesser to a human birth. As described in the sūtras, wholesome deeds that are nonetheless carried out with an impure attitude lead to birth as a demigod.

The correlated effect involves an experience similar to the cause. Here it means that the experiences that were mentioned above during the unwholesome deeds are now transformed into their opposite harmonious factors. *The Jewel Garland* describes this:

> To have a long life, wealth, and no enemies,
> To be praised, famous, and to hear pleasant words,
> To have your word honored, your wishes fulfilled,
> To have ease of mind, and superior intelligence
> Are the ten effects similar to their wholesome causes.

The correlated effect also involves a behavior similar to the cause, which means that in the future one will enjoy and take pleasure in the same actions that one has done previously.

Finally, the dominant effect ripens in one's environment in the following ways:

> Nutritious crops, good harvests, a pleasant environment,
> Land free from bumps and with fertile soil,
> Lush vegetation, and timely seasons,
> Grains thick and flavorful, and fruit trees in bloom
> Are the dominant results of the ten wholesome deeds.

It is therefore essential to resolve that if we can live by the ten wholesome deeds, it will lead us to happiness both in this life and in the next, and for that reason we must carry them out to the best of our ability.

Neutral actions, like eating, walking, and moving around are actions done with no particularly positive or negative attitude, and so a particular pleasurable or painful effect cannot be determined. However, through neutral acts we waste our time, squandering and rendering useless our freedoms and advantages. So it is therefore necessary to transform neutral acts into positive ones. This can be done if we aspire toward the pure conduct described in the sūtras. To do that we must form a strong resolve, starting today, to transform all our actions into wholesome ones, so that they do not just remain petty and meaningless. In particular, we must embrace all physical, verbal, and mental activities with the mind of awakening. *The Four Hundred Verses* speaks of this:

With the attitude of the mind of awakening,
Any deed, wholesome or not, is suitable—
Transformed as it is into virtuous goodness.
The power of a kind heart makes this possible.

In *The Way of the Bodhisattva*, it says:

Even when I am asleep or careless,
From today onward, the strength of merit
Will be uninterrupted and manifold,
Reaching to the end of space.

Do not pay attention to external things but keep your focus inward. Strive in the art of turning all that you do into the path of wholesome deeds.

Reflecting on the Nature of Trust: A Conclusion in Terms of the Four Truths

Aśvaghoṣa spoke of the benefits of trust in the following verse:

The precious wheel of trust will guide us
Day and night on a wholesome path.

If our trust in cause and effect is stable, we will naturally feel enthusiastic and determined to do good. Trust is especially important for beginners as it inspires us toward good deeds and away from negative acts. On the other hand, if we lack trust, the teachings will not be able to benefit our minds and we will remain like a boulder in the depths of the ocean. We will also not be able to cross the ocean of cyclic existence, like a boat without a steersman. Neither will we understand the words or the meaning of the teachings, like a blind person going into a temple. The sprout of enlightenment will also not be able to grow, like a seed that has been burned by fire. Moreover, it will be impossible to free ourselves from suffering, like a sheep that has fallen into a pit.

Finally, we will be left empty-handed, although we possessed the freedoms and advantages, like a person without hands traveling in a land of gold. A sūtra mentions the importance of trust:

> No positive qualities emerge
> In those who lack trust,
> Just as a sprout does not grow
> From a seed burned by fire.

On the other hand, for those who have trust it is a wonderful quality. Like fertile soil, it brings all excellent yields. Like a wish-fulfilling jewel, it fulfills any need or wish. Like a king who maintains the law, it establishes everyone in happiness. Like a well-guarded castle in a place where danger looms, it keeps out faults and secures all good qualities. Like a boat that crosses a wide river, it frees us from the suffering of birth, aging, sickness, and death. Like a guide in a dangerous place, it frees us from the dangers of cyclic existence and the lower realms. It is therefore vital to gain trust in the principle that actions have consequences. *The Collection of Good Advice* speaks of this:

> The one who has the greatness
> Of the correct view of the world,
> Will not go to the lower realms
> Even during a thousand eons.

Now, the four truths are objects that one can feel confidence in, and they can be explained according to the following analogies. The truth of origin is like food and behavior that cause a sickness. The truth of suffering is like being afflicted by the pain of the sickness. The truth of the path is like relying on a remedy, such as medical treatment as well as proper food and behavior. The truth of cessation is like using that remedy to recover and get well. Similarly, being encumbered by miserliness is the truth of origin. To become poor and destitute is the truth of suffering. To practice generosity is the truth of the path. To dispel, through generosity, the suffering of poverty in the future is the truth of cessation. In this way, all types of cause and effect can be understood.

In short, although all beings possess the essence of the thus-gone ones, the luminous nature of mind, they do not recognize it due to coemergent ignorance. Because of conceptual ignorance, they make distinctions and conceive the aggregates to be a person and phenomena to have a self. This in turn gives rise to all disturbing emotions, such as attachment. Subsequently, the disturbing emotions lead to wholesome, unwholesome, and nontransferring karma. This is how the result—the universes, beings, aggregates, and elements of the three realms—manifests. Here, the karmic aspect of the truth of origin and the definition of the truth of suffering should be understood in the way it was explained above.

To remedy this situation, the cause is to awaken one's potential, while the condition is to be accepted by a spiritual teacher. The method is to rely on his or her instructions and generate the roots of virtue that accord with liberation. This means to practice the complete and unmistaken path that unifies means and wisdom by forming the awakened attitude of the great vehicle and training in the meaning of the two types of selflessness. In this way, the objects of purification—all the stains of saṃsāric phenomena, which are temporary and appear while being nonexistent—gradually come to cease. Finally, one will then actualize the ultimate truth of cessation, the buddha of the three bodies that is present within the ground, along with its enlightened activity.

This is a unique and profound instruction that shows how pure causes lead to pure effects in dependent origination. Once we understand it, we must strive, in any way we can, toward the unexcelled accomplishment of the path of the great vehicle. The Buddha himself offered this advice to his followers:

> I have shown you the path of liberation,
> But know that liberation depends on you.

This concludes the general instruction on generating the attitude of renunciation.

Planting the Seeds of the Special Preliminaries

The root text says:

> If you wish to gain the common and supreme accomplishments
> in this life,
> First, ripen your mind with empowerment and keep your
> commitments pure.
> Then, go for refuge, the root of the path,
> And arouse the twofold mind of awakening, the essence
> of the path.
> Then, perform the profound practice of Vajrasattva,
> To purify all misdeeds and obscurations that prevent
> Experience and realization of the vajra vehicle, the consummate
> path.
> Next, to perfect conducive conditions, the accumulations
> of merit and wisdom,
> Offer the ocean of pure realms of the three bodies as a
> maṇḍala.
> Especially, apply the key points of devotion
> In guru yoga, the core of every path.

Thus, the special preliminaries have five aspects: (1) taking refuge, the root of the path of liberation, (2) arousing the mind of awakening, the essence of the path of omniscience, (3) practicing the meditation and recitation of Vajrasattva to purify adverse conditions, misdeeds, and obscurations, (4) offering the maṇḍala to perfect the favorable conditions of the two accumulations, and (5) practicing the guru yoga of blessings, the ultimate aspect of the path of the vajra vehicle.

Taking Refuge

All paths that make good use of the freedoms and advantages originate in the practice of going for refuge. There is a verse that speaks of this:

> You may have received all the vows
> Yet, without taking refuge, have none.

On a temporary and causal level, our objects of refuge are the Three Jewels in the way that they have manifested in someone else's stream of being. We go for refuge in these objects since these Three Jewels are able to protect us from the fear of cyclic existence and bring us to the unsurpassed fruition, which is liberation. *The Sūtra of Mañjuśrī's Perfect Emanation* mentions this:

> I take refuge today in the Buddha,
> The Dharma, and the assembly of the Saṅgha,
> Who dispel the fears of the frightened,
> And protect those without a refuge.

In this context, the Buddha refers to the four bodies and the five wisdoms. The Dharma is that of the great vehicle, which is peaceful, beyond attachment, and teaches the truths of cessation and the path. The Saṅgha is that of the noble nonreturning bodhisattvas.

In the resultant vajra vehicle of secret mantra, on top of these three we add the guru, whom we seek for blessings, the yidam deity, whom we seek for spiritual accomplishment, and the dharma protectors, the wisdom beings who aid us in accomplishing enlightened activities. It may seem that this all adds up to six, but in fact, the guru is the embodiment of all the Jewels, the yidam deity is the Buddha, and the wisdom ḍākinīs and dharma protectors can be included as part of the Saṅgha. We can also add representations of these objects of refuge, such as statues, scriptures, and stūpas, as well as all ordinary and noble beings who follow either the lesser or the greater vehicle. This would include members of the Saṅgha who abide on the paths of accumulation and joining according to the great vehicle, as well as listeners and solitary buddhas.

Our ultimate and absolute refuge, nonetheless, is exclusively the dharma body of the Buddha because it is the final realization of the path of training. *The Supreme Continuum* mentions this in the following verse:

> In ultimate truth, the Buddha
> Is the single refuge of beings,
> For the Sage has the dharma body,
> And is also the highest in the assembly.

According to the sūtra path, the Buddha's dharma body is the fruitional refuge that one strives to accomplish, at a future time, in one's own being. In the unique approach of the vajra vehicle, however, the Buddha's dharma body is understood to be the essence of mind, which is already enlightened right now, an embodiment of all the Jewels.

In general, going for refuge is necessary for anyone who wishes to train on the paths of the three types of beings. In the present context, however, one must also have an affinity for the great vehicle and a wish to enter the resultant vajra vehicle of secret mantra. The reason for taking refuge is to be saved from three types of fear. In general, one fears the suffering of cyclic existence. In particular, for followers of the great vehicle, there is a fear of selfishness. Most specifically, for followers of secret mantra, one fears ordinary, deluded fixation. Moreover, one should continue taking refuge until one has reached enlightenment—until the ultimate three objects of refuge manifest in one's stream of being.

The way to take refuge is to accept the Buddha as one's teacher. We do so because he shows us the profound path to liberation of which we would otherwise be unaware. We also accept the Dharma as the path because by practicing it according to the Buddha's instruction, we are freed from all fears and directly connect to the final fruition. In certain contexts of the extraordinary vajra vehicle, taking refuge in the Dharma also refers to taking refuge in the sense of making a commitment. One commits to perfecting the realization of the pure channels transformed into the emanation body, the pure energies transformed into the enjoyment body, and the pure essences transformed into the dharma body; or, otherwise, perfecting the realization of the indivisible essence, nature, and compassion. In this way, we are promising to rely on all the teachings of the paths of the nine vehicles. Finally, we rely on the Saṅgha as our companions because by emulating their conduct, we will be able to arrive at our destination.

To take refuge merely due to a personal wish for the higher realms or tranquility is the path of the lesser and middling vehicles and should therefore be avoided. Instead, we should take refuge while engendering the attitude of the great vehicle, in order to have a support and ally in liberating all beings from existence, and to allay all obstacles on the path of the great vehicle. *The Ornament of the Sūtras of the Great Vehicle* says:

> One commits due to a wish for the real and realizes it
> through compassion.

By taking refuge in the Three Jewels and pledging ourselves to them, we implicitly also make a commitment to give up their antitheses, such as powerful worldly gods, religions that encourage violence, and extremist friends who have a negative view and behavior.

Once we have achieved certainty about the general principles of taking refuge, the actual practice is to visualize as follows. Imagine yourself in a vast and expansive pure realm, adorned with innumerable beautiful features. In the sky before you is a wish-fulfilling tree made of a variety of precious substances, with exquisite foliage, flowers, and fruits, and stretching out through all of space. It has a central branch and four other branches extending out in the cardinal directions. In the middle of the central branch is a lion throne that supports a lotus, a sun, and a moon disc. On this throne sits the master from Uḍḍiyāṇa, the knower of the three times. In essence he is your root guru, but his appearance is that of the glorious subjugator of appearance and existence. Surrounding him on all sides are the lineage masters.

On the branch in front are the hosts of yidam deities of the four and six classes of tantra in all their infinite peaceful and wrathful manifestations. On the branch to the right of the guru are the buddhas of the ten directions and three times including our teacher, the Lord of Sages, all in the form of supreme emanation bodies. On the branch behind is the jewel of the Dharma—the truth of cessation and of the path—in the form of scriptures stacked high as a mountain. On the branch to the left is the Saṅgha of the great and lesser vehicles—the bodhisattvas as well as the noble listeners and solitary buddhas. Surrounding these and in all the space between are the protectors of good—the ḍākinīs, dharma protectors, wealth gods, and treasure guardians—gathered like cloudbanks.

In the presence of all of these objects of refuge, you should visualize your father and mother on your right and left respectively, clearly as though they were actually there. In front of you are your enemies, including those who have harmed you, along with your friends and all other sentient beings without distinction, gathered like a crowd in a market place. All of you together pay respect physically by joining your palms together and making prostrations. You pay respect verbally by chanting the verse of refuge in a collective hum. You pay respect mentally by thinking, with heartfelt longing and tears in your eyes, "You are aware of whatever I and all sentient beings do. From now until I reach enlightenment, in this life and in future ones, I have no other hope or refuge besides you." In this way, chant one hundred thousand times along with the amending number the refuge verse:

> Namo!
> I and all sentient beings equal to space take refuge
> In the guru, Buddha, Dharma, and Saṅgha, and the hosts
> Of yidams, ḍākas, ḍākinīs, and Dharma protectors,
> In all who are endowed with great compassion.

It is ideal if you can complete one hundred thousand prostrations as well, either along with this or later when you practice the seven branches.

At the end of the session, imagine that as a result of your yearning devotion, light rays stream out from the bodies of the objects of refuge and strike all sentient beings, cleansing and purifying them of all misdeeds, obscurations, faults, failings, and stains, transporting them instantly to a pure realm. The field of accumulation melts into light and dissolves into the main figure, Guru Rinpoche, who also melts into light and dissolves into you. At this point give up fixation on the idea that the objects of refuge and your own mind are different and remain as long as you can in that nonconceptual state, which is beyond expression. This is the ultimate refuge, the natural state.

When you emerge from that, dedicate the goodness and then engage only in daily activities that are meaningful. Embrace them with mindfulness, attentiveness, and conscientiousness, without contradicting the refuge precepts, including the three categories of things to avoid, to practice, and the supplementary trainings. The benefits of taking refuge are described in a sūtra:

> If the merit of taking refuge
> Had a physical form,
> It would fill up all of space,
> And then surpass it.

And also:

> Whoever goes for the triple refuge
> Will swiftly attain buddhahood.

Arousing the Mind of Awakening

The instruction on arousing the mind set upon supreme enlightenment, the essence of the path of omniscience, is threefold: (1) arousing the mind of awakening in aspiration, (2) gathering the accumulations, and (3) applying the mind of awakening through mind training.

The Mind of Awakening in Aspiration

In this short life when our time of death is uncertain, there are many ways to make use of the freedoms and advantages. However, the core of them all is to arouse the mind set upon supreme enlightenment. It says in *The Essay on the Mind of Awakening*:

> Without arousing the mind of awakening,
> You will never attain enlightenment.
> There is no other way in saṃsāra
> To benefit yourself and others.

At the heart of the mind of awakening is the wish to attain complete enlightenment for the sake of others. It says in *The Ornament of Realization*:

> Arousing the mind of awakening is to wish for
> Complete and perfect enlightenment for others' sake.

The mind of awakening springs forth out of immense love and compassion with the objective that all sentient beings attain complete enlightenment. Supported by altruism—the courage to take on the burden of the welfare of all sentient beings—it is in essence the wish to achieve enlightenment, and thus the power to liberate all beings.

Based on the degree of bravery, there are three kinds of resolve. The incomparable resolve, like a shepherd, is the wish to become enlightened oneself only after having first establishing all other sentient beings in that state. The resolve of true wisdom, like a ferryman, is the wish for oneself and all sentient beings to attain enlightenment at the same time. The resolve of great ambition, like a king, is the wish to first become enlightened oneself and then afterward establish all sentient beings in that state. These three can also be summed up in the two aspects of compassion that is directed toward sentient beings and insight that is directed toward complete enlightenment. All the other ways we may classify them can be included in aspiration and application.

Here, arousing the mind of awakening in aspiration means the wish to attain awakening; it is like preparing for a trip. Arousing the mind of awakening in application means to actually engage in the bodhisattva conduct, the methods for becoming awakened; it is like actually going on the trip. It says in *The Way of the Bodhisattva*:

> In brief, we should understand
> That the mind of awakening has two aspects:
> The mind of awakening in aspiration,
> And mind of awakening in application.
>
> The wise should understand the difference
> Between the two, which form a sequence,
> Like the difference between intending to go
> And actually going on a trip.

The way to actually arouse the mind of awakening is to reflect as follows:

> In general, wherever the basic space of phenomena pervades, space pervades as well, and as far as space pervades, there are sentient beings. Every one of them has been my mother and father in lifetimes without beginning; there is not a single exception to this. In that role, just like my present mother and father, they produced my body, gave me life, and later taught me the ways of the world, helping me out as much as they could in so many immeasurable ways. They saved me from countless dangers, strove to make me equal to my peers and then, if I was equal, to put me ahead. To state it simply, they had only immense kindness for me and cherished my life more than their own.
>
> All of them want only happiness, but without knowing the means to achieve it, they create only the causes of suffering. How sad that sentient beings are so lacking in happiness and helpless in their suffering! But what does it help to leave my "compassion" at this? I ought to help them out myself. But right now I don't have the power to do that. So from this day on, I will work toward gaining supreme enlightenment

> for the sake of others, just as the buddhas and bodhisattvas of the past have done. I will take on the burden of liberating all the infinite beings until cyclic existence is entirely emptied. No matter what happens, I will not give up, but will keep my mind set on unsurpassed enlightenment.

With this in mind, visualize the field of accumulation as described before and accumulate one hundred thousand recitations of the verse for arousing the mind of awakening:

> HOḤ
> Just as in the past the conquerors along with their children
> Aroused their hearts toward unexcelled supreme enlightenment,
> I too will accomplish buddhahood to benefit
> All mother sentient beings as far as space pervades.

Gathering the Accumulations

In the presence of this same extraordinary field of accumulation, make prostrations along with all sentient beings, while imagining that you have emanated as many bodily forms as there are dust particles in the world. Make offerings, both of material goods and by imagining the ocean-like offering clouds of Samantabhadra. With regret and sorrow, admit to every negative, harmful deed you have carried out in all your lives without beginning until this one, both by doing things that are inherently wrong and by violating the three vows after taking them. Then pledge to refrain from them again in the future. Rejoice with a joyful heart in all the goodness, ordinary or supreme, that exists in saṃsāra, nirvāṇa, or the path. Then turn to the buddhas, bodhisattvas, teachers, and spiritual friends who have accomplished their own benefit and have the capacity to benefit others in an immense way. Request them to compassionately consider the endless ocean of beings in need of guidance. Urge them to turn the unsurpassable wheels of the vast and profound Dharma, and furthermore to remain in their form bodies throughout countless millions of eons without passing into nirvāṇa. Then think, "Just as the buddhas and bodhisattvas of the past have done, I fully dedicate all the goodness I have accrued throughout the three times—exemplified by this practice of the seven branches—toward the essence of unsurpassed enlightenment for the sake of all beings." With this strong determination, accumulate either ten thousand or one hundred thousand recitations of the verse for gathering merit, the seven branches:

> OṂ ĀḤ HŪṂ HRĪḤ
> I prostrate to the knowledge holder Padmasambhava
> And all objects of refuge in the ten directions.
> I present Samantabhadra clouds of offering,
> Material and imagined, filling the sky.
> I confess breaking and transgressing the vows of
> individual liberation,
> The bodhisattva trainings, and the knowledge holders'
> tantric bonds.
> I rejoice in all the noble and the ordinary beings,
> Who carry out the conduct of the victors' children.
> Please turn the appropriate wheels of Dharma
> In order to relieve the pain of infinite beings.
> Please don't pass beyond sorrow, but for the sake of beings
> Remain for immeasurable millions of eons.
> I dedicate all virtue gathered throughout the three times
> So that all beings may attain the very heart of enlightenment.

The Mind of Awakening and Mind Training

Śāntideva, the son of the conquerors, has said:

> If merely wishing to alleviate
> The headache of every sentient being
> Is a helpful frame of mind
> That brings countless merit,

What need to speak of striving for
The happiness of countless beings?

In *The Sūtra Requested by Śrigupta* it is said:

Whoever joins his palms and turns
To the buddhas in the ten directions,
To prostrate and present them offerings,
To rejoice in every merit,
To confess all his misdeeds,
To supplicate and pray to them—
The mass of merit created through this
Will forever fill up all of space.

The amount of merit that is accumulated by taking refuge, arousing the mind of awakening, and offering the seven branches for the sake of others is beyond measure and limit. To have then the unwavering wish to give all your causal virtues—as exemplified by the merit you have just gathered—as well as your resultant happiness to sentient beings so that they may reach the sublime happiness of the state of enlightenment is "love." "Compassion" is the wish that all the suffering of other sentient beings, both causal and resultant, will ripen on you, thus freeing them from suffering and its causes. "Joy" is the wish that all sentient beings will always be genuinely happy, beyond suffering. Finally, "great equanimity" is to be without bias in the realization that everything within saṃsāra and nirvāṇa, whether friend or foe, has the nature of equality. Therefore, bring to mind a heartfelt resolve to actualize these four states while training in the mighty conduct of the heirs to the Victorious One. Then chant as much as possible the verse:

By this merit may all sentient beings have happiness.
May they be free from suffering and may their suffering ripen
upon me.
Never separated from the happiness free of suffering,
May they abide in equanimity, the equality of all things.

The extensive way is to accumulate one hundred thousand of each of the verses for aspiration, gathering the accumulations, and application. The medium way is to accumulate as many as one can, for example ten thousand of each. The concise way would be to accumulate as many as possible, ten thousand or so, of just the verse for aspiration since the application is also implied in that.

When concluding, absorb the field of accumulation into yourself. Then recognize that in truth there is no subject, object, and action—no beings toward whom the mind of awakening is aroused, no one arousing it, and no manner in which it is aroused. Within that recognition, settle evenly into the state beyond concepts, the ultimate mind of awakening, the nature free of conceptual constructs; then dedicate the merit. During session breaks, always make your experience meaningful by remembering the virtues and precepts of the mind of awakening.

The Meditation and Recitation of Vajrasattva

Whichever realm of existence we are born into, we are not beyond suffering, the root of which is the truth of origin—karma and disturbing emotions. As it says in *The Jewel Garland*:

> Desire, aggression, and delusion
> Create unwholesome karma.

Also it says in *The Way of the Bodhisattva*:

> Suffering, unhappiness,
> The various types of fear,
> And lacking what we want
> Are caused by negative deeds.

Therefore we should quickly apply the methods of purifying negative deeds. As it is said:

It may come that I must die
Before I've purified my misdeeds.
Please, now, save me quickly
So I am liberated from them.

The antidote, the way to purify our negative deeds, is to confess and apologize. If we conceal our misdeeds and keep them secret, we add the water and fertilizer of hypocrisy to the seeds of wrongdoing that we have already planted. By doing so, they will only grow stronger. On the other hand, if we do not hide our wrongdoings, but acknowledge our mistakes and disclose them, their force can never increase and instead will only lessen. In this way, "confessing" means to openly and directly divulge our faults to the person to whom we are apologizing. "Apologizing" is to concede, with sincere regret, that an action was wrong. A true apology should be made in a heartfelt way by first admitting one's many faults and showing one's shame and embarrassment. Then, by earnestly confessing, we must ask the person to whom we are apologizing to accept us out of love and so purify us of our negative karma.

For this, it is necessary to bring together the four powers, which form a special remedy. These are mentioned in *The Sūtra on the Teaching of the Four Principles*:

> Maitreya, when a bodhisattva possesses four principles, he can overcome any misdeeds he has committed and gathered. These four principles are the application of total remorse, the application of the antidote, the power of restoration, and the power of the support.

If we can apologize by employing all four powers in the remedy, we can be sure that all our negative deeds will be purified in this life. Nāgārjuna has said:

Whoever was careless in the past,
But later becomes conscientious
Is as beautiful as the moon in a cloudless sky,
Like Nanda, Aṅgulimāla, Ajātaśatru, and Udayana.

In the special context of the secret mantra vajra vehicle, the meditation and recitation of Guru Vajrasattva is a practice that fully purifies all negativity and obscurations, like scattering a hundred birds in one instant. Within it, all four powers are brought together.

First comes "the power of the support," which refers to visualizing the deity. After first taking refuge and arousing the mind of awakening, you should visualize a lotus and a moon disc above you, in your ordinary form. Upon the moon disc, indivisible from your guru, is Vajrasattva, the transcendent conqueror who embodies the wisdom of all the buddhas of the three times. He is white in color with one face and two arms, the right hand holding a vajra, and the left a bell. He is in union with Vajratopa, the consort who manifests from his own radiance. She is white and holds a knife and skull in her hands. Both are in the prime of youth, have the major and minor marks complete, and are adorned with silks and jeweled ornaments. The male figure sits in the vajra posture and the female in the lotus posture. Together they sit amidst an expanse of rainbows, orbs, and masses of light.

"The power of total remorse" means to arouse sincere regret and sorrow due to the shame and panic that one feels for the negative actions and downfalls that one has previously committed, like that of someone who has ingested poison. The "power of resolve" means to think that, from now on, even at the cost of one's life, one will not commit such negative acts again.

Preceded by these, "the power of applying the antidote" is to imagine as follows. In Guru Vajrasattva's heart center is a moon disc. In the center of this disc rests a white HŪṂ syllable, the spiritual life-force of all the bliss-gone ones, surrounded by the chain of the one-hundred-syllable mantra. By reciting the one-hundred-syllable mantra in either its long or condensed form, it emanates light, making offerings to the noble ones and clearing away sentient beings' obscurations. It is then reabsorbed, and from the seed syllable and the mantra chain, white nectar pours down like a stream of milk, entering you through the crown of your head. Like a rushing cascade that carries silt along with it, all of your negativity, obscurations, damaged and broken vows, faults, and downfalls, in the form of pus, blood, insects, liquid ash, and charcoal, come out from your sense doors and even the pores of your skin as a black liquid. In this way, you are cleansed and purified, and your body becomes transparent and stainless like a crystal ball. As the stream of milklike nectar completely fills you up, think that the qualities of experience and realization take birth effortlessly in your stream of being. Chant aloud starting with, "ĀḤ Above my head, on a lotus and moon . . ."

In particular, recite the one hundred syllables one hundred thousand times along with the amending number and the six syllables as much as possible.

When you conclude the session, if you would like to and are able, supplicate with the *Lamenting Apology*, starting with "HOḤ Great compassionate Blessed Vajrasattva . . ." If that is not possible, supplicate with the lines starting, "Protector, due to my ignorance and lack of understanding . . ." Continue to the point where Vajrasattva smiles and says, "Child of noble family, all your negative deeds and obscurations are purified." Imagine that he thus absolves you, and with great joy, melts into light and dissolves into you, so that all your negative deeds and obscurations are purified, and your damaged and broken vows are restored. Then settle in the unfabricated natural state, which is the most superior way of purification. This is mentioned in a sūtra that says:

> Whoever wants to practice repentance,
> Should sit straight and look into reality.
> Looking at reality as it really is,
> Reality is seen, and you are free.
> This is the supreme repentance.

Also, a sūtra describes the merits of persevering in this practice:

> The one who has done something harmful,
> But later undoes it with goodness,
> Illuminates the world like the sun
> Or the moon in a cloudless sky.

The Tantra of Realization in Three Words says:

> The one who meditates on Vajrasattva
> And carries out the recitation of his mantra
> Will purify every negative action,
> And become like Vajrasattva himself.

The Maṇḍala Offering

The maṇḍala offering is a practice that perfects the accumulations and gathers conducive circumstances. It is important to make this offering diligently with the conviction that actions ripen into particular effects; it is a profound method that swiftly accomplishes an immense accumulation of virtue. A tantra speaks of this:

> Offering every billionfold realm
> Ornamented with all desirable things
> To the enlightened beings in all their realms,
> Enlightened wisdom will be perfected.

Likewise, a sūtra says:

> For those with merit, every wish is fulfilled.

In general, the unexcelled practice of the bodhisattvas is to accumulate merit and wisdom. Through merit and wisdom, we are able to clear away all stains that obscure the three bodies, which are the ultimate fruition. Likewise, merit and wisdom are what allow us to manifest the two bodies and so benefit others and ourselves abundantly. Here, in the context of the preliminaries, we should strive to gather the two accumulations by means of the maṇḍala offering. Normally, unless by chance in previous lives we have gathered the accumulations in an extraordinarily vast way, our stream of being will not have a firm foundation in the accumulation of virtue. Without that foundation, even though we may have a propensity for virtue, it may not ripen immediately, and so it will be difficult to swiftly gain experience in the main practice. Moreover, even if we do manage to gain a little experience, it will be a slow and fragile process, and we may not be able to make real progress. If, on the other hand, we accumulate virtue anew in an extraordinary way, it will awaken our spiritual potential and propensity for virtue, and we will quickly gain strong experience and realization. Therefore, we should be diligent in maṇḍala offering, which is a simple and profound method for quickly perfecting the two accumulations.

To do this, first arrange the accomplishment maṇḍala with five heaps and then visualize the field of accumulation as in the previous description of the objects of refuge. As for the offering maṇḍala, it is said that if it is a supreme one made of a precious metal such as gold or silver, it should be at least four inches wide. If it is made of something on the level of bronze, it should be at least one span. If it is made of a lesser material such as clay or wood, it should be at least a forearm's length. If you cannot acquire any of these, even a flat piece of stone will suffice. The material you use for the heaps should at best be precious stones, second best medicinal herbs and incense, or third best grains and the like. Moreover, if you can afford it, you should not merely add replenishments, but actually switch the offering substances each time. However, if that is too expensive, you must at least replenish the offering substances. In any case, it is very important to use clean substances and not be tainted by stinginess.

The actual way to offer is to combine three aspects into one: physically, offer the heaps; verbally, recite the verse of offering; and mentally, perform the visualization.

The outer maṇḍala, then, is to offer the outer vessel—the billions of external universes, each composed of the four continents, Mount Meru, the sun, and the moon—as well as the inner contents that fill them up, the immeasurable wealth of gods and men. Offer these mentally, like the bodhisattva Samantabhadra did in his prayer, so that from each world more world systems emanate until they are as numerous as drops in the ocean. The inner maṇḍala is to offer, without a care or regret, everything in your possession—your aggregates and sense bases, your dear and cherished wealth, as well as the virtue you've accumulated throughout the three times, so that you and all other sentient beings may complete the accumulations of merit and wisdom. The secret maṇḍala is to offer all of this in a way that is sealed by the view that does not conceptualize in terms of subject, object, and action.

Someone with a sharp mind will be able to offer these three maṇḍalas simultaneously, but if that is not possible, you can alternate between them. In any case, be sure to accumulate one hundred thousand of the extensive maṇḍala offering up to and including its mantra:

> OṂ ĀḤ HŪṂ
> The bodies, enjoyments, and every virtue
> Of myself and the infinite sentient beings,
> Four continents, Mount Sumeru, the sun, and the moon,
> The inconceivable riches of gods and men,
> Samantabhadra's great clouds of offerings,
> Which I emanate unceasingly,
> I continuously offer with veneration
> To the precious Three Jewels as well as the three roots,
> To the ocean of dharma protectors and wealth gods.
> Perfecting the great accumulation of merit,
> May the illumination of wisdom spread.
> OṂ GURU DEVA ḌĀKINĪ SARVA RATNA MAṆḌALA
> PŪJA MEGHA ĀḤ HŪṂ

If you cannot do that, accumulate ten thousand as well as one hundred thousand of the concise maṇḍala verse from the Tara practice, along with its mantra:

> OṂ ĀḤ HŪṂ
> The three realms, worlds, beings, splendor, and riches,
> My body, enjoyments, and every accumulation of virtue,
> I offer to the lords of compassion.
> Please accept them and bestow your blessings.
> OṂ SARVA TATHĀGATA RATNA MAṆḌALA
> PŪJA HOḤ

You should also supplicate for your desired aims, so that the extraordinary qualities of experience and realization may take birth in the mind-streams of yourself and others, and so that everyone may swiftly attain the precious state of enlightenment. At the end of the session, dissolve the field of accumulation along with the offering materials into yourself and settle evenly without holding anything in mind. Afterward, dedicate the merit. During session breaks, you should persevere in the many ways of gathering the accumulations, such as prostrating, circumambulating, and making offerings and donations.

A tantra speaks of the benefits of this type of offering:

> Carrying out the wholesome practice of the maṇḍala is diligence.
> Removing any bugs and creatures is the best forbearance.
> Cleansing and wiping the maṇḍala is enlightened discipline.
> Anointing it with medicine and perfume is generosity.
> Placing flowers on top is insight.
> Visualizing it as the deity is concentration.
> Inviting, welcoming, prostrating, offering, and circumambulation are methods.
> Clearing the two obscurations and perfecting the two accumulations are power.
> Attaining the fruition of this practice is wisdom.
> Knowing that it will benefit others is aspiration.
> Thus, the meaning of the maṇḍala completes the perfections.
> Therefore, strive diligently in maṇḍala offering.

Guru Yoga

The practice of the guru yoga of blessing is the ultimate path of the vajra vehicle. It is divided into three aspects: (1) the outer practice in the manner of supplication, (2) the inner practice in the manner of recitation and receiving empowerment, and (3) the innermost practice of the true guru yoga of simplicity in the manner of activity application.

The Practice of Supplication

The attainment of supreme liberation, the ultimate truth of cessation, along with the qualities of enlightened activity—the manifestation of the three bodies—rests on receiving the guru's blessings, the consummation of the path. Acknowledging this, we should strive in the guru yoga of devotion. As it says in *The Avataṃsaka Sūtra*:

> All of the bodhisattva's aspirations come from the spiritual friend.

Also, *The Condensed Realization* explains:

> The guru is more exalted
> Than the buddhas of a thousand eons,
> Because all of those eons of buddhas
> Came about by relying on gurus.

Nāgārjuna has said:

> When someone is falling from a mountain peak,
> He may wish not to fall but will still keep falling.
> If by the guru's grace, you gain supportive instruction,
> You may think you won't be free but will still be liberated.

Thus, in general, all the qualities of the path of the great vehicle rest on the principal condition of the spiritual friend. In particular, in this context of the unsurpassed secret mantra, the main part of the path and the root of all practice is to bring to mind the features of the guru's enlightened body, speech, and mind, and focusing on that, to train with constant devotion. The rationale for this is explained in all the sūtras and tantras, which say that one's own root guru is a buddha manifest. In terms of qualities, he or she is no different from all the buddhas. Yet, in terms of kindness to us, the guru's kindness is actually even greater than that of the buddhas. This is also described in scriptures, such as

The Vajra Mirror:

> The guru is Vajrasattva, lord of the maṇḍala,
> Equal to all the buddhas.

In *The Sūtra of Immaculate Space* it is mentioned:

> Ānanda, a thus-gone one does not appear to all beings, but spiritual friends do; they teach the Dharma, and plant the seeds of liberation. Therefore, understand that a spiritual friend is superior to the thus-gone ones.

The Tantra of the Secret Assembly says:

> Having the same nature
> In constitution and activity,
> The guru is equal to all the buddhas.
> Yet in showing others the path,
> He is much superior to the Buddha himself.

Therefore, resolve that your own root guru is the essential embodiment of every refuge. Consider anything he does to be part of the enlightened activity of guiding beings. Remember with gratitude his kindness, so that your mind is seized by devotion and you feel an overwhelming longing for him. In this way, you can transform your mind and, by continuously remembering him in this way without distraction, bring a halt to ordinary experience. Therefore, be diligent in practicing guru yoga with a heartfelt devotion that has these four special qualities. For the actual practice, first visualize the support. Then chant the lines:

> Amid an ocean of offering clouds in the sky before me,
> On a layered lion throne, lotus, sun, and moon,
> Is Urgyen Tötreng Tsal, embodiment of all refuge objects.
> With one face, two arms, and a wrathful smile, he glows
> with brilliance.

He wears the lotus crown, inner dress, gown, dharma robes, and brocade cloak.
His right hand holds a vajra, his left a skull and vase,
And he embraces the secret seal in hidden form as a khaṭvāṅga,
His two legs in reveling posture in a sphere of five-colored rainbow light.
He sends out infinite cloudbanks of the three roots.
Appearance and existence is the essence of the glorious guru.

Imagine that the place where you are, instead of the way it ordinarily appears, is replete with all the features of the unexcelled realm of the Lotus Net. Then, in the sky before you, among a gathering of oceanlike clouds of exquisite offerings, is a lion throne that supports a seat made of a lotus, a sun, and a moon. This is where your root guru sits. In essence he is the embodiment of every refuge, yet he appears in the form of Urgyen Tötreng Tsal. He is white with a rosy complexion, has one face and two arms, is wrathfully smiling, and glowing majestically. On his head he wears the lotus crown, and his body is bedecked with a secret dress, a gown, Dharma robes, and a brocade cloak. He holds a vajra in his right hand and a skull with a nectar-filled vase in his left. With the crook of his left arm he embraces his secret consort in the hidden form of a khaṭvāṅga staff. With his two legs in the playful royal posture, he sits amidst an expanse of five-colored rainbow light. From the main places of his body, he projects and absorbs cloudbanks of countless maṇḍalas of infinite deities belonging to the three roots. All of appearance and existence is the nature of the guru's vajra body, speech, and mind. Like a ball of sesame seeds, it is filled with the oceanlike maṇḍala wheels of the objects of refuge—the Three Jewels and the three roots.

Then, in order to receive swift blessings, imagine all of this while you chant, with deep-felt devotion and yearning, the prayer *Clearing Obstacles to the Path*. You should chant this prayer as much as you can, such as a thousand or ten thousand times. Afterward, make sure to chant the short prayer, *Buddha of the Three Times*, one hundred thousand times. In any case, at the beginning of each session, first chant

Clearing Obstacles to the Path either seven or twenty-one times, as it suits you, and then go on to accumulate the short prayer. If you like, you can also insert lineage supplications, such as *Bestower of the Splendor of Accomplishments.*

The Practice of Recitation and Empowerment

Imagine that your heartfelt and devoted supplications cause the three bodily places of the assembled deities to project rainbows, lights rays, orbs, deities, seed syllables, and symbolic implements, countless like dust particles in a sunbeam. These all dissolve into you, granting you every empowerment, blessing, and accomplishment without exception. Then perform the recitation of the VAJRA GURU mantra. Ideally, you should repeat it ten million times. Second best is to chant it one million two hundred thousand times, but at the least you should complete four hundred thousand recitations. When concluding the session, chant:

> From the four places of the body of the glorious guru
> Light emerges and dissolves into my four places.
> By blessing me with vajra body, speech, mind, and wisdom,
> I obtain the four empowerments.

At this point, all the retinues of the three roots dissolve into the great master of Uḍḍiyāṇa, who is the embodiment of every refuge. Then, from the four places of his body—his crown, throat, heart, and navel—appear white, red, dark blue, and multicolored lights, which in essence are the vajra body, speech, mind, and wisdom of all buddhas. As the light dissolves into your four places, you obtain the vase empowerment, the secret empowerment, the wisdom-knowledge empowerment, and the suchness empowerment. This purifies the four obscurations related to the waking state, the dream state, deep sleep, and immersion. Thus, you are empowered for the practice of the development stage, inner heat, consort practice, and the luminous great perfection. In this way, you become destined for the fruition of the emanation body, the enjoyment body, the dharma body, and the essence body. With this in mind, rest evenly in the true meaning of empowerment.

The True Guru Yoga of Simplicity

Recite the verse:

> The great master of Uḍḍiyāṇa
> With great joy dissolves into me.
> In the state of the unfabricated all-ground,
> My mind, free from fixation,
> Is the pure dharma body devoid of constructs.

Then, imagine that your deep-felt devotion causes the great master of Uḍḍiyāṇa to appear above your head, where he joyfully melts into light and dissolves into you. At this point you should rest evenly while looking into the natural face of innate empty awareness, free from any concepts of the three times. This is the essence of uncontrived wakefulness in which your body, speech, and mind mingle indivisibly with the guru's three secrets, like water mixed with water. Afterward, train in the main practice of the development and completion stages. Alternatively, if you are returning to your daily activities, dedicate the root of goodness to the heart of enlightenment and seal with pure aspirations, chanting:

> HOḤ
> In the circle of the vast display of the basic space of phenomena,
> The virtue of practicing the secret mantra of the great vehicle
> Together with all virtue gathered throughout the three times,
> I dedicate toward the heart of unexcelled enlightenment.
>
> By this merit may all obstacles—outer, inner, and secret—
> For all of the infinite beings come to cease.
> Reaching the end of their travel on the path of the two stages,
> May they swiftly attain the state of the Lotus King.

Always pass the time during session breaks with activities that are in accord with the Dharma and never part from the devotion of focusing on the guru as your path. The benefits of being diligent in guru yoga are described in *The Precious Assemblage Tantra*:

> Compared to meditating for hundreds of thousands of eons
> On the forms of hundreds of thousands of deities,
> It is better to remember the guru, even briefly,
> For the merit of doing so is boundless.

Moreover, no matter which practice you are focusing on, make sure to go through the entire preliminaries once each session, from refuge through to guru yoga. Also, if you are doing a short recitation retreat and wish to do a condensed version of the preliminaries, it is said that one can begin by chanting the refuge verse ten thousand times while doing an equal number of prostrations. Then, chant the verses for the mind of awakening as much as you can. Subsequently, gather ten thousand recitations of the hundred-syllable mantra, the long or the short maṇḍala offering, and the short supplication for the outer practice of guru yoga, respectively. Then, if possible, perform one thousand recitations of *Clearing Obstacles to the Path*. Lastly, gather four hundred thousand of the inner practice of the VAJRA GURU mantra. At the conclusion of every session, do the innermost practice of sustaining the view.

This concludes the explanation of the special preliminaries.

The Main Practice

The explanation of the main practice has three parts: (1) an explanation of the development stage, corresponding to the form of the enlightened body, (2) an explanation of mantra recitation corresponding to enlightened speech, and (3) an explanation of the completion stage corresponding to the luminous enlightened mind.

The Development Stage: Enlightened Body

The root text explains:

> All phenomena, both relative and ultimate,
> Are the superior great dharma body, the two truths
> inseparable.
> Through the practice of great emptiness, the basic space
> of suchness,
> The luminous natural state is realized at death.

This explanation consists of (1) establishing a framework with the three samādhis, the cause, (2) developing the maṇḍala of the support and supported, the fruition, and (3) training in holding the appearance of the deity, the main object of focus.

The Three Samādhis

The samādhi of suchness is to acknowledge, as it has just been described, that all phenomena of saṃsāra and nirvāṇa are primordially pure and perfect within the great and extraordinary dharma body, which is the natural equality of the union of the two truths. Then, feeling certain that this is how things are, rest evenly in the state of unity free from constructing thoughts. Be confident in the thought "Death in its pure form is the dharma body." This samādhi purifies the death state and fosters the seed for manifesting the dharma body. It also ripens you by laying the foundation for the actual luminosity to take birth in your mind-stream on the higher path of the completion stage.

For the samādhi of total illumination, without wavering from that state of emptiness, cultivate great compassion—a compassion that is beyond any reference point and pervades all of space—for the beings who have not realized it. Be confident in the thought, "The intermediate state in its pure form is the enjoyment body." This samādhi purifies the intermediate state and establishes the link for perfecting the fruition of the enjoyment body. It also ripens you by laying the foundation of great compassion, which is the cause for emerging out of luminosity as the unified form of the deity.

For the causal samādhi, meditate in a mind-state of clarity and steadiness on your awareness as the white syllable HRĪḤ, the natural expression of the unity of emptiness and compassion. Be confident in the thought, "The birth state in its pure form is the emanation body." This purifies the birth state and establishes the link for manifesting the fruition of the emanation body out of the enjoyment body. It also ripens you for the completion stage, in which you arise as the form of the deity out of blissful energy.

The Support and the Supported Deities

The root text explains,

> Purify miraculous birth by visualizing it complete in an
> instant's recall.
> Purify heat birth by visualizing the seed that projects and
> absorbs.
> Purify womb birth with the seed, the implement, and body.
> Purify egg birth with the causal and resultant heruka.
> In any case, visualize the maṇḍala of the support and the
> supported,
> Complete with face, arms, and details.

I will explain here four ways of visualizing to purify the habitual patterns of the four types of birth, just as they are taught in the great tantras in general. First, in order to purify miraculous birth, is the way of "completeness in an instant's recollection." Here, one should not apply effort by gradually developing the maṇḍala as in the lower vehicles, but instead take up the view of the ati vehicle that the maṇḍala is spontaneously complete without effort, with no need to develop it. Thus visualize the entire maṇḍala of the support and supported complete in an instant's recollection, like a fish leaping out of water. Master Ganthapāda has said,

Meditate without any seed,
Like a being taking birth miraculously.

Second, to purify birth from heat and moisture, is the "simple style of visualization." Here, take up the view of the great anuyoga scriptures, according to which all things are by nature pure and perfect as the fundamental maṇḍala of awakened mind—the great bliss child, nondual basic space and wakefulness. Thus cultivate the maṇḍala of support and supported by merely uttering the essence mantra. It says in *The Magical Key to the Treasury*:

In the anuyoga vehicle, without developing it,
But merely uttering the essence mantra,
The visualization is complete.

Third, to purify womb birth, is the ritual of the three vajras. I will not elaborate on it here since it will be explained below. Fourth, to purify egg birth, are the elaborate ways of visualization, the rituals connected to *your children* and *another's child*.

For the ritual of *your children*, it is explained that you, being already a buddha, make others your children. Here, "you" means the nature of awakened mind, which is enlightenment free from beginning or end. This is what every buddha emanates out of, and so all the thus-gone ones can be said to be its children. To practice this, first cultivate the three samādhis, and then imagine that out of the seed syllable and the symbolic implement appears in the sky the causal heruka with one face and two arms.

For the ritual of *another's child*, it is taught that in order to spontaneously accomplish your potential so that it does not diminish, you should make yourself another's child. This means that although the nature of the awakened mind is to be primordially enlightened, if you are not blessed by a spiritual teacher and do not gain possession of self-aware wakefulness, you will not manifest as an enlightened being. Therefore, you should make yourself the child of the thus-gone ones. To practice this, first visualize that from the heart center of the heruka in space, seed syllables project, producing the gradually stacked four elements, the central mountain, the celestial palace, and the throne. The causal heruka is then requested to descend on the throne and, by the song of invocation, melts into light, becoming an orb of the nectar of awakened mind. From this emerges the body of the resultant heruka. Then, as if giving birth, the deities in the retinue appear from the cloud of the nectar of awakened mind at the union of the secret places of the male and female deities.

According to the tantra and sādhana sections, there are three ways of visualizing: elaborate, medium, and concise. Among these, the present explanation has followed the medium approach to visualization according to the system of the sādhana section. An individual should practice these four styles progressively in accord with his capacity, as the All-Knowing Dharma Lord has said,

> Though there are four ways to meditate, you should use
> The one that addresses the type of birth that predominates.
> To purify habitual patterns, meditate accordingly using them all.
> In particular, meditate in harmony with egg birth as a beginner,
> And when this is somewhat stable, with womb birth.
> Once very stable, meditate in harmony with heat-moisture
> birth,
> And when completely habituated, use this true stability
> To develop instantaneously, in harmony with miraculous birth.

Among these approaches, I will here explain the ritual of the three vajras, which purifies womb birth. This has three parts: visualizing the support, the celestial palace and the throne; visualizing the supported, the main deity and retinue; and sealing by blessing the three places and bestowing empowerment.

Visualizing the Support

Visualize the seed syllable HRĪḤ, hovering in space. This syllable emanates the syllables RAṂ, YAṂ, and KHAṂ, which purify clinging to the world and beings as real. Reabsorbing, the vajra protection dome is formed, spacious and vast. Within that dome, the syllables E, YAṂ, RAṂ, BAṂ, and LAṂ are projected. Starting from below, they respectively produce the maṇḍalas of space, wind, fire, water, and earth along with the central mountain. On top of the mountain, the syllable BHRŪṂ is projected, which in turn becomes the celestial palace of wisdom jewels. It is square, with four gates, causal and resultant architraves, and so on. As the Great Unexcelled Realm of the Lotus Net, it is perfectly complete in every detail and proportion and glows with rainbows, orbs, and masses of light. Inside, there is an eight-faceted jewel and a four-petaled lotus, in the center of which is a seat made of a lion throne, lotus, sun, and moon. All this should be visualized clearly.

The specific details of the palace and the seat, as well as descriptions of the objects of purification and the processes of purification are explained thoroughly in *The Luminous Jeweled Lamp: A Summary of the Main Points of Approach and Accomplishment* by the vajra holder, Kongtrul Rinpoche. They are also described in the supplement for that text, which I composed, *The Luminous Jeweled Mirror*. Since these details are listed in those texts, I have not included them here.

Visualizing the Supported

First comes the enlightened speech ritual of the seed syllable, in which the seed syllable HRĪḤ descends onto the throne. Next follows the enlightened mind ritual of the symbolic implement, in which the seed syllable becomes a vajra, the symbolic implement of the buddha family. Finally, there is the ritual of the complete enlightened body, in which the vajra projects and absorbs light rays, carrying out the twofold benefit, before becoming a mass of light from which you appear in the form of the deity. In this way, the naturally existing wisdom awareness that primordially transcends bondage and liberation appears symbolically in the form of Padmasambhava, embodiment of all the bliss-gone ones.

His complexion is white with a rosy hue, he has one face and two arms, and his expression is of peacefully smiling wrath. He wears on his head the lotus crown that liberates upon sight. His body is bedecked with the layers of the secret dress, gown, dharma robes, and brocade cloak. His right hand brandishes a five-spoked vajra in the gesture of pointing in threat. His left hand holds a skull filled with nectar and a jeweled life-vase in the gesture of equanimity. In the crook of his left arm he holds his sublime secret consort Mandarava in the hidden form of a khaṭvāṅga staff. With his two legs in the playful royal posture, he sits in an expanse of rainbows and orbs of five-colored light.

Above him, on top of a lotus stem, sun, and moon seat, is the enjoyment body, Avalokiteśvara, white, with one face and four arms. With his upper two arms he joins his palms at his heart center. His lower right hand holds a crystal rosary, and in his lower left hand he holds the stem of a white lotus. Above him is the dharma body, Amitābha, or Amitāyus, with a red body, one face and two arms. With his hands in the gesture of equanimity, he holds a vase of nectar. These two, the dharma body and enjoyment body forms, are endowed with all the silk and jewel enjoyment body ornaments and are sitting with their two legs crossed in vajra posture.

Around them, on the anthers of the four-petaled lotus, are four emanations. To the east is Gyalwey Dungdzin, whose body is white. He holds a sword in his right hand and a hook in his left. To the south is the radiantly white Mawey Senge or Vādisiṃha, who holds books in the gesture of expounding the Dharma. To the west is the yellow Kyechok Tsulsang, holding a vajra in his right hand and a jeweled box in his left hand in the gesture of equanimity. To the north is the light brown Dukyi Shechen, supporting at his hip a recitation dagger in his right hand and aiming an activity dagger at the obstructers with his left.

Surrounding them, on the eight-faceted jewel, are another eight emanations. To the east is the dark blue Dzamling Gyenchok, wielding an activity dagger with both hands. To the south is the brilliant blue Pema Jungney, holding a vajra and bell crossed at his heart, and embracing his consort, the white princess. To the west is the radiantly white Khyepar Pakpey Rigdzin, showing the path with a vajra in his right hand, and using a three-pronged khaṭvāṅga as a staff with his left. To the north is the maroon Dzutrul Tuchen, holding a vajra and dagger.

To the southeast is the knowledge holder Dorje Drakpo Tsal, holding a vajra and scorpion, and embracing his consort Vajra Vārāhī. To the southwest is the dark blue Kalden Drendzey, holding a vajra and skull with blood, in union with his consort Namshelma. To the northwest is the dark maroon Rakṣa Tötreng, holding a vajra and skull with blood, embracing his consort Ting-ö Barma. To the northeast is the bright red Dechen Gyalpo, holding a vajra and bell and embracing his consort. As the self-display of great wakefulness, they are all replete with the appropriate peaceful or wrathful expressions, ornaments, and attributes to guide those in need.

Surrounding them, on lotus and sun thrones at the four doors, are the four attendant ḍākas with their consorts, each the color of one of the four activities. In their right hands they hold knives marked with their particular symbol, and in their left hands they hold skulls. They are adorned with jewelry and bone ornaments and stand in dancing posture with one leg bent and one extended. In addition, imagine that all the space outside, inside, and between is entirely filled—like the sky dense with clouds or the sun and its rays—with an oceanlike gathering of knowledge-holding masters, the three roots, and dharma protectors. As an inconceivable display of the magical net, they guide whomever is in need.

Blessing and Bestowing Empowerment

Visualize that, at the crown of all the deities in the visualization, there is a white OṂ, the nature of the vajra body and the purity of earth and water. In their throats there is a red ĀḤ, the essence of vajra speech and the purity of fire and wind. In their hearts there is a dark blue HŪṂ, the nature of vajra mind and the purity of basic space and mind. In this way, their body, speech, and mind are originally present as the essence of the three vajras.

Empowerment deities filling up the sky then bestow empowerment on them, so that the five disturbing emotions are cleared away and the five wisdoms take birth in their mind-streams. As the purity of the five aggregates, their crowns are ornamented with the bliss-gone ones of the five families, presided over by the chief of their family. The empowerment deities then dissolve indivisibly into these. If you wish, carry out the invitation, offering, and praise according to the liturgy. However, if you simply seal with the view of realizing that the samaya beings and wisdom beings are originally inseparable, you are not leaving anything out. As it says in *The Two Segments*,

> The deity is you and you are the deity.
> You and the deity are coemergent.
> So there's no need to invite, nor request to remain.
> Visualize your mind as the divine master.

The Appearance of the Deity

The root text says,

> At first, to gradually gain familiarity,
> Visualize your body in the single form,
> Vividly appearing like the colors of a rainbow.
> At best, see its nature as the great reality.
> Next best, visualize it with details clear and distinct.
> At the least, remain absorbed in the stake of unchanging realization.
> Place a painting with all the correct features before you,
> And focus on it with one-pointed mind, eyes, and breath.
> When a clear image appears, drop all faults of agitation and dullness,
> Rest on the deity's form of unified emptiness and appearance,
> And experience the calming of churning thoughts.
> At times, leave consciousness at ease in its natural state.
> At times, transform the displays of samādhi in different ways.
> Every session, bring out the deity's vivid appearance in fullness.
> Every session, plant the great stake of the essence mantra.

Every session, rest in the one taste of your mind and the deity.
Every session, practice the magical displays of projecting and absorbing light rays.
Always take pride in being no different from the deity.
To join ground and fruition through the path of unity,
Train in total purity, which stops clinging to ordinary experience.

This part consists of (1) vivid appearance, (2) stable pride, and (3) recollection of purity.

Vivid Appearance

All phenomena within appearance and existence—the outer universe and the inhabitants within it, the aggregates, elements, and sense bases—are primordially perfect as the maṇḍala of bodies and wisdoms. Visualize them appearing vividly, like a moon reflected in water, as the maṇḍala of support and supported, the display of the magical net guiding whomever is in need. As you do this, keep in mind all the general and specific details.

If it is difficult to visualize them clearly in your mind, place a painting that has correct proportions in front of you and practice with that as a support. Cast aside the mistakes of agitation and dullness. At times, relax while sustaining the recognition that the deity's form is the display of your own mind. Using the general instructions on development stage such as these, practice with assiduousness. When the experiences of clarity and stability manifest, cultivate your strength in samādhi by sealing with the methods of letting all appearance and activity emerge as the infinitely pure circle of the deity by means of projecting and absorbing it all as the forms of the deities. In this way, exert yourself in becoming more proficient.

Stable Pride

All phenomena of saṃsāra and nirvāṇa are nothing other than the expression of natural awareness. There is no deity to be found outside of your mind and no mind to be found apart from the deity. The indivisibility of your mind and the form of the deity is the fundamental great bliss, primordially beyond bondage and liberation, the ultimate, naturally existing Lotus King. Stable pride means to recognize and feel inalienable conviction that this is the way things are. If you know how to bring this confidence onto the path and are able to, it is a genuine short cut. So cultivate the attitude, "I myself am the guru of the fruition, the three bodies of enlightenment, along with my retinue—the state in which all flaws are exhausted and all qualities perfected."

Recollecting Purity

In order that your development stage practice does not stray into materiality, but enacts a transformation into authentic wakefulness, keep in mind its meaning, the purity of its symbolism, as follows. At the time of the ground, all that is conceptually formed—sentient beings' aggregates, elements, and sense bases—are primordially pure as the form of the deity. At the time of the fruition, the display of the magical net of the vajra bodies of all the buddhas manifests to guide whomever is in need for as long as existence lasts.

Representing this as the supreme lord of the maṇḍala is the Lotus King. He has the single face of having perfected all aspects of the ground within the single sphere of simplicity. He has two arms that represent the unity of method and insight, thus all the aspects of the path. His two legs are in the playful royal posture since he has realized all aspects of the fruition through the equal taste of existence and peace and because he does not abide in any extreme. His body is the white color of being untainted by the obscuration of dualistic experience, subject and object, and has the rosy hue of compassion and affection for beings. He is glowing majestically with an expression of peacefully smiling wrath on his face since he manifests in limitless ways to guide the endless ocean of beings in whichever way necessary.

He wears the white secret gown of spontaneously perfecting all superior qualities without abandoning saṃsāra and the ways of a householder but instead taking them onto the path. Over that he wears the patterned blue brocade gown of possessing the three secret treasuries of the tantras, statements, and instructions. It is fastened with his vajra belt, which binds all concepts into immutable great bliss. As the lord of the teachings of the three collections, he wears the red dharma robes with yellow patterns, which symbolize having completed the three trainings and reached the end of the path of aspiration and application. He wears the maroon brocade cloak of bringing all beings under his influence and overwhelming them with his brilliance. On his head he wears the azure-colored lotus crown as a symbol of empowerment, having perfected the four great streams of empowerment. Having perfected the nine vehicles, his crown is adorned with a vajra top-ornament, as well as with a mirror, peacock feather, and silk streamers, signs of indivisible basic space and wakefulness in which the five bodies are spontaneously present.

His right hand is raised in the sky and holds the five-spoked golden vajra of empty appearance, which represents thought being inseparable from the deity and the perfection of the vase empowerment. As a symbol of having perfected the secret empowerment, with his left hand in equipoise, he holds the skull cup of the basic space of emptiness, filled with the nectar of awakened mind. As a symbol of having perfected the knowledge empowerment, there is a life-vase of immortality within the skull cup, full of an elixir representing the wisdom of the four joys, empty bliss. As a symbol of having perfected the fourth empowerment, the lid of the life-vase is adorned with a jewel that fulfills wishes spontaneously and without effort.

In the crook of his left arm he supports a khaṭvāṅga staff, which is the hidden form of the consort, who is the seal of the basic space of great emptiness replete with all the supreme qualities. As a symbol of having perfected the empowerment of the display of awareness, the khaṭvāṅga staff has three prongs, representing the three gates to complete liberation as well as the three aspects of essence, nature, and compassion. It has three heads—one a dry skull, one fresh, and one shriveled—that symbolize the three bodies. It is also adorned with various decorations, such as silk ribbons, which symbolize that beings are guided through unified means and knowledge. Since he is unrivalled in his majesty and has perfected all qualities, such as the ten powers and four types of fearlessness, he sits on a lion throne. Being untainted by flaws like attachment, he sits on a lotus and, having unified means and knowledge—bliss and emptiness—he sits on a sun and moon seat.

Above him is Avalokiteśvara, the one who shakes saṃsāra from its depths. He is the identity of vajra speech and, in the context of the ground, this refers to the channels and elements abiding as the cloudlike wheels of syllables and all sounds and utterances being nonarising empty sound. In the context of the fruition, the identity of vajra speech means that cloudlike wheels of syllables are emanated from the chakras of the enjoyment body buddhas. They purify the worlds in the ten directions as well as the obscurations of the six classes of beings and show the inconceivably infinite gateways to the Dharma according to their needs.

Being unstained by any fault or flaw, Avalokiteśvara is white in color. He has the one face of the single taste of the bodies and wisdoms. He has four arms to tame beings with the four boundless qualities. The first two of them are joined with palms together at his heart as a symbol of emptiness, the unity of everything within saṃsāra and nirvāṇa. With his lower two arms he holds a crystal rosary since he proclaims the sounds of Dharma to beings, and a white lotus since he is untainted by flaws. He sits with his legs in the vajra posture, representing the realization of the equality of existence and peace.

He wears a silken upper garment, which represents eradicating the misery of suffering, and a skirt that symbolizes being unstained by disturbing emotions. He is adorned with jewelry, which symbolizes the perfection of supreme qualities and the ability to fulfill all hopes, whatever is needed or wished for. Having perfected the five wisdoms, he wears the crown of the five buddha families. As a symbol of his great compassion, he wears a deerskin over his left shoulder.

Above him is vajra mind, the dharma body buddha Amitāyus, who is the lord of the family. At the time of the ground, he is awareness, awakened mind, primordially beyond bondage and liberation and the foundation for all undefiled qualities. At the time of the fruition, he is undefiled basic space, free of every obscuration, which forms the basis for the manifestation of the bodies and wisdoms. His body is red, symbolizing his affection for beings and discriminating wisdom. He has the one face of the single sphere of simplicity. With the gesture of equanimity his two hands, representing the union of basic space and wakefulness, hold a vase full of the nectar of immortal wisdom. Not dwelling in the extremes of existence or peace, his legs are in vajra posture. He is adorned with all of the silk and jewel ornaments since he has purified the eight collections of consciousness in themselves and manifested the five wisdoms.

Then there are the twelve manifestations of the Guru, representing the twelve sense bases being naturally purified at the time of the ground, and at the time of the fruition, the manifest realizations of the twelve truths, the pure identity of the twelve links in reverse order. The four gate-keeping ḍākas with their consorts symbolize the four possible eternalist and nihilist concepts being naturally purified at the time of the ground, and at the time of the fruition, the four demons being conquered within basic space, as well as the taming of beings through the fourfold enlightened activity.

Integrate the recollection of the purity of the maṇḍala of support and supported in this way as much as you can. To condense it to the crucial point, all the supreme qualities of buddhahood are naturally and spontaneously present within the genuine intrinsic nature. Out of this, the qualities appear in symbolic form as the features of the maṇḍala of support and supported. We should therefore understand that it is the defining characteristic of all the phenomena of the indivisible ground, path, and fruition to be primordially pure. It is of course essential to recollect this purity when meditating according to the practice manual.

Specifically, in this context, one should first sincerely recall the purity of each and every aspect. Having done that, one should enter one-pointedly in samādhi that joins the divine pride with the clear appearance of the deity. In this way, the deity you visualize appears while being devoid of any intrinsic nature. There will be bliss, but no attachment, and clarity, but without concepts. The deity's essence is the dharma body, its appearance is the enjoyment body, and its identity is the myriad magical emanations of the emanation body.

By training in this way in bliss, clarity, and emptiness, the two accumulations will be swiftly completed. Gradually becoming more adept, you will perfect the five experiences of movement, attainment, familiarity, stability, and completion. As well, you will reach three levels of clarity. First, the deity will appear as an object of mind, secondly as an object of the senses, and finally, when you master the deity, it will appear in others' perception. In this way, you will capture the thousandfold life-force of all of saṃsāra and nirvāṇa, accomplish true speech, and your energetic mind will mature into the subtle body. Based on the support of the matured knowledge holder, you will arrive at the level of a knowledge holder of the great seal. This is mentioned in the root text:

> From one-pointed practice you will experience movement,
> Attainment, familiarity, stability, and completion,
> Gain the three levels of clarity, and meet the form in actuality;
> What you say will come true, your realization immutable.

This completes the explanation of the development stage corresponding to the form of the enlightened body.

Mantra Recitation: Enlightened Speech

The explanation of mantra recitation, which corresponds to enlightened speech, covers (1) the recitations for the three bodies, (2) the combined accomplishment, and (3) the activity application.

The Recitations for the Three Bodies

This section covers the recitations of (1) gathering blessings for oneself based on the dharma body, (2) the all-pervasive activity for others based on the enjoyment body, and (3) unified development and completion, with no distinction between self and other, based on the emanation body.

The Recitation of the Dharma Body

First open the recitation mansion and invoke the deities for the recitation. Then, above both the self- and front-visualizations, visualize the syllable HRĪḤ in the heart center of Amitāyus, the lord of the family. This syllable emits light rays that stream out in the ten directions and gather back all your vitality and life energy that has been lost, has lessened, or has dissipated. On an outer level, the light rays also gather the essences of the elements—earth, water, fire, and wind. On an inner level, they bring back the vitality, merit, power, and ability of the beings of the three realms. Finally, on an innermost level, the lights gather the wisdom qualities of the buddhas and bodhisattvas—their knowledge, compassion, and power.

All of this is gathered back in the form of five-colored nectar, which streams into the vase in his hands. As the nectar begins to boil, it flows down through the crown of your head, completely filling your body. In this way, the four obscurations are purified, you attain empowerment and accomplishment, and obtain the vajra life force of immortality. Then, perform the recitation while keeping all of this in mind.

If counting by number, accumulate four or twelve hundred thousand of the mantra. If counting in terms of signs, it is said that these should include meeting the deity in actuality, hearing its voice, and attaining the heat of samādhi. However, these signs could also refer to a variety of actual and meditative experiences, such as seeing a sun or moon rising, acquiring a representation of enlightened body, speech, or mind, drinking nectar, or seeing a river overflowing.

The Recitation of the Enjoyment Body

In the heart center of the noble guide of beings there is a white HRĪḤ syllable, supported by a lotus flower and a moon disc. Visualize that the six petals of the lotus are marked by the six syllables of his mantra. Then, as you recite the mantra, the syllable HŪṂ projects dark blue light, the essence of mirrorlike wisdom, to the hell realms. It dispels the cause of being born there, aggression, and the result, the suffering of heat and cold. In this way, it transforms the environment and inhabitants in their entirety into the realm and bodily forms of the noble ones of the vajra family.

In the same way, the syllable ME emits yellow light, the essence of the wisdom of equality. It dispels the hungry spirits' avarice, as well as their hunger and thirst, and transforms the environment and inhabitants into the pure realm of jewel family beings. The syllable PAD projects white light, the essence of the wisdom of the basic space of phenomena, which dispels animals' delusion, stupidity, and dumbness, and establishes them in the realm of the noble ones of the bliss-gone family. The syllable ṆI sends forth the red light of discerning wisdom that dispels the desire, busyness, and dissatisfaction of humans, transforming them into the realm of lotus family beings. The syllable MA projects the green light of all-accomplishing wisdom, which dispels the envy, quarreling, and strife of demigods, transforming them into the realm of the activity family beings. The syllable OṂ emits white light, the nature of the wisdom of luminosity, which dispels the gods' pride and their suffering of having to die and descend, transforming them into the realm and bodily forms of noble beings who embody all families.

Finally, the syllable HRĪḤ projects infinite light rays, which are the essence of the wisdom of indivisibility. These rays dispel the karma, disturbing emotions, and suffering of all sentient beings and transform them all into the bodily forms of the noble guide of all beings. Imagine that all sights, sounds, and thought activity transform into the body, speech, and mind of the Great Compassionate One, so that the activity of stirring cyclic existence from its depths is completed. With all of this in mind, carry out the recitation of the seven syllables. If counting by number, accumulate ten million recitations. The signs are said to include having visions of the Noble One, either in actuality, a vision, or a dream, as well as giving rise to impartial compassion.

The Recitation of the Emanation Body

You are the mahāguru who embodies all buddha families. Visualize that in your heart center is a five-spoked vajra, supported by a moon disc. In its hub is another moon disc, on top of which rests the syllable HRĪḤ, white and glowing. Surrounding this syllable is the VAJRA GURU mantra chain, white in color and self-resounding, spinning uninterruptedly in a clockwise direction. Fix your attention on this visualization, which is like a moon with a garland of stars. That is the intent of approach, as it invokes the mind of the deity.

From this mantra chain, a second mantra chain streams out without any interruption. It emerges from your mouth and enters the mouth of the wisdom being in front of you. Circulating through his body, it emerges from his navel and reenters you through your navel. Then, once again, it proceeds from your heart center and continues to circle as before. Imagine that subtle luminous nectar gathers in your heart-sphere, stabilizing the wakefulness of great bliss and bringing the two types of spiritual accomplishment within your control. This recitation, which is likened to a spinning firebrand, is the intent of close approach as it brings you close to the deity.

Next, the mantra circle emits countless light rays, which spread to infinite buddha realms. There, they transform into outer, inner, and secret offering clouds that please the three roots as well as the victorious ones and their children. The blessings of their three secrets are then gathered back and dissolve into you, so that the two obscurations are purified, the two accumulations are completed, and you obtain every empowerment, blessing, and spiritual accomplishment without exception. Then, once again, light rays are projected. The light rays strike all sentient beings in the three realms and purify their obscurations of karma and disturbing emotions as well as their related habitual patterns. This visualization, which is like a king's messengers being dispatched, is the intent of accomplishment because one gains mastery of the attainment of the spiritual accomplishments.

Finally, the outer vessel of the universe becomes the unexcelled vajra realm. All its inhabitants are the maṇḍala deities, all sounds of the animate and inanimate world are the self-resounding sound of mantra, and all thought-activity is the play of great naturally existing wisdom. To carry out the recitation in this way, within the vast state of appearance and existence as manifest ground, is a practice described as a broken beehive. It is the intent of great accomplishment since the spiritual accomplishments are actualized.

The tantra tradition teaches that these four intents of recitation primarily should be combined with the single form, the elaborate form, and the group gathering practice respectively. It is also said that one should go through them in a progressive manner where one first attains vivid appearance in the samādhi of the level one is at before moving on to the next. In this context, however, according to the intent of Guru Rinpoche's pith instructions, the four intents of recitation relating to approach and accomplishment are combined in a single session. This is a profound technique for swiftly giving rise to the signs of blessing and spiritual accomplishment.

If counting by number, recite the root VAJRA GURU mantra, which encompasses all the buddha families, one million two hundred thousand times. If counting by signs, it is said that you will meet the deity or hear his voice—either in actuality, a vision, or a dream. It is also said that your body will become blissful, your speech powerful, realization will dawn in your mind, and that ḍākas and ḍākinīs will gather around you.

Combined Accomplishment Practice

After carrying out the recitation in this way, visualize that all the deities in your maṇḍala and those in the recitation mansion in front emanate numerous forms identical to themselves, filling all of space. They perform vajra songs and dances and, while not wavering from the realization of the luminosity of enlightened mind, they send out an inconceivable number of offering clouds, pleasing the infinite victorious ones and their children. Their enlightened activity magically manifests an unimaginable number of forms that guide beings according to their need, and in this way they dispel sentient beings' obscurations. Bestowing empowerment upon them with the nectar of awakened mind, all beings awaken as the forms of the three roots. At times "mount the horse" of the melodious tune. Recite as many of the TÖTRENG TSAL mantras as possible, for instance, four hundred thousand times. If you like, you can also perform the profound inner HŪṂ practice and the secret recitation of great bliss according to their visualizations in *The Recitation Manual.*

The Recitation for the Activity Application

If you prefer, you can follow *The Recitation Manual* and practice the recitation of each of the four ḍākas individually. However, if you prefer the brief version according to the practice manual itself, the visualization is as follows. Imagine that light rays project out from the heart centers of the chief figures—both yourself and the one in front—invoking the minds of the ḍākas of the four classes. The ḍākas then pervade every universe with emanations and re-emanations that spontaneously accomplish all the pacifying, enriching, magnetizing, and wrathful activities. With this in mind, practice the HA RI NI SA recitation, just a tenth of the amount of the main mantra.

During all of these recitations, it is important to chant clearly, with your attention undistracted from the various visualizations, such as projection and absorption. Thus, perform the recitation within the continuity of audible emptiness—nonarising and beyond fixation—while recognizing the indivisibility of deity, mantra, and reality itself. *The Tantra of the Emergence of Cakrasaṃvara* mentions this:

> The mantra is the form of the yoginī;
> The yoginī is the form of the mantra.
> Whoever strives for the sublime state,
> Do not divide them in two!

Also, the Great Master of Uḍḍiyāṇa has said,

> Recite with undistracted concentration.
> Should you become distracted elsewhere,
> Even reciting for an eon will bring no result.

Therefore, persevere in mantra recitation. Regardless of which aspect of recitation you were focusing on, when the time comes to complete the session you should chant the verses for the offerings and praises as well as the supplication *Clearing Obstacles to the Path*. Then, proceed according to the recitation manual with such practices as admitting mistakes, receiving the empowerments, and dissolving the recitation mansion into yourself. The root manual summarizes this:

> The intent of recitation for these is as follows:
> Both the samaya maṇḍala of oneself
> And the front maṇḍala of the wisdom deity
> Have a mantra garland at their heart center.
> As you project light, it invokes the front visualization,
> Which in turn projects and absorbs light rays.
> Thus the accomplishments are attained as described.
> At the end, everything dissolves into your heart.
> If you train in this type of practice
> In a state of clear samādhi,
> You will come to see the maṇḍala circle firsthand,
> Hear the sound of the vajra mantra,
> And reach the level of heat in yogic discipline.
> At the least, you will experience in your dreams
> The signs as they have been described before,
> And the individual activities will be accomplished.
> Have no doubt that you will achieve the signs.

This completes the explanation of mantra recitation, corresponding to enlightened speech.

The Completion Stage: Enlightened Mind

The root text explains:

> The practice of dissolving within ultimate luminosity is as follows:

Utter HŪṂ HŪṂ HŪṂ so that the universe, inhabitants, and your body
Successively dissolve into the spiritual life force, the syllable HRĪḤ.
Without holding even that in mind, rest in the innate state of luminosity.
The past has vanished, the future not yet come,
While present awareness is utterly open.
Settle in that state, with mind looking into mind.
At that time, whatever thoughts may arise,
They are all the play of the one nature of mind.
Just as the nature of space does not change,
You see the nature of mind to be changeless and all-pervasive.
This is the consummation of all vehicles, the Great Perfection,
The unsurpassed, self-existing state of the mind section.
Whoever engages in this ultimate practice
Will manifest the secret signs and boundless qualities,
Gradually perfect the great strength of experience and realization,
And achieve the wisdom of ever-excellent Padma.

When the time comes for completing a session, prepare for the dissolution by visualizing the indivisible samaya and wisdom maṇḍalas. As you utter HŪṂ three times, all of appearance and existence, the universe and inhabitants, melt into light and dissolve into the celestial palace and the deities. The deities dissolve successively into the central figure, the central deity into the spiritual life force of the vajra, and the vajra into the syllable HRĪḤ, which gradually dissolves into basic space, where nothing is held in mind. Look directly into your natural face and settle evenly within the state that is beyond grasping at appearance and awareness.

Your present awareness—where past thoughts have ceased and future ones have not yet arisen—is wide open and beyond any word and expression. Its essence is empty so there is nothing to hold in mind. Its nature is cognizant so it is spontaneously present. Its compassion is all-pervasive and unceasing. This is the realized state where the three enlightened bodies are primordially beyond being lost or gained. It is true reality, which is not found elsewhere. It is your own awareness—naturally existing wakefulness. It is limitless and unrestricted like the sky; indescribable since words cannot define it; inconceivable since consciousness cannot know it. Being beyond any extreme, it is the great equality of simplicity.

Its essence is unchanging throughout the three times. By its nature there is no quality to accomplish and no fault to remove. This is the natural and innate state of the ground. Although it is beyond the realm of conventional thoughts and statements, you resolve on it from within, without mistakenly ascribing reality to it, excitedly thinking that it exists (or doesn't exist) in a particular manner. It is precisely this present and unfabricated wakefulness that is the true, naturally existing Padmasambhava.

Therefore, without falling into assumption and pretense, investigate thoroughly and recognize it for yourself. Resolve that apart from this, there is no quality to cultivate, no deity to accomplish, and no practitioner who accomplishes it. When you rest in this state, various pleasant and displeasing experiences may arise as it expressions. However, they all arise within this reality, abide within it, and are freed within it. As such, they are naturally arising and naturally liberated, like rainbows in the sky or waves on the ocean. You can therefore feel confident that nothing can affect the basic nature for better or for worse, and persist in the natural practice, which is like the flow of a river. *The All-Creating Monarch* mentions this:

> Listen! I am the all-creating king, awakened mind—
> In me there is nothing to embellish or deny.
> So without making thoughts or meditating at all,
> Leave your three doors as they are, uncontrived.
> Whatever arises is naturally liberated.
> Unborn and beyond direction like space,
> Know that I am the natural Great Perfection.

And also,

> Uncontrived naturalness is the nature of everything—
> Apart from this nature, there is no other buddha.
> To use the word 'buddha' is just to label it.
> The nature is nothing other than this mind.
> This mind, unfabricated, is called the dharma body.
> Unfabricated, it has never been subject to birth.
> Beyond birth, it cannot be found or created.
> It is not made or produced through seeking and creating.

And as well,

> The one who abides in nondoing,
> May have the ordinary body of a god or human,
> But his mind is the buddha, reality itself.

When you arise from this state or are returning to your daily activities:

> Say PHAṬ PHAṬ PHAṬ and view the whole universe
> And its inhabitants, including yourself, as the maṇḍala circle.
> In the state of unified development and completion,
> The two accumulations, merit and wisdom, will unfold.

As it says here, utter PHAṬ three times, whereby you arise as the deity. Then bring all appearances and activities onto your path as the play of the great bodies and wisdoms. In all the breaks between your sessions, strive to bring your training onto the path whether you are practicing the development stage or the completion stage. In this way, carry the state of equipoise into the ensuing attainment and train in developing your capacity.

I have composed these notes on the first level of practice based on the earlier teachings of the two vajra holders concerning the preliminary practice liturgy and the instructions on approach and accomplishment. As the root text for these notes, I used the section on the development stage from the chapter of "The Quintessence of Unimpeded Wisdom," found in *The Essence Manual of Oral Instructions*. Moreover, I extracted the vital points from the elaborate and condensed practice manuals as well as *The Recitation Manual* and further adorned it with the teachings of the great beings of the past.

At its conclusion, it would have been suitable to provide an explanation on the general completion stage practices, combined with the six completion stage teachings of Guru Viśuddha Heruka as they are taught in *The Essential Meaning of Unimpeded Great Bliss*. However, I was unable to do so since I have never received the lineage of its profound instructions. Moreover, you should learn to practice the path of the extraordinary Great Perfection—the thorough cut to primordial purity and the direct crossing to spontaneous presence—according to the instruction manual *Sphere of Refined Gold*, composed by the precious master, the omniscient vajra holder.

The oral teachings of the knower of the three times, Uḍḍiyāṇa,
Are the essential extract of ten million tantras, statements, and instructions.
In accord with them all, yet superior to them all,
Is the marvelous treasury of secret instructions, possessing the six liberations.

My mind, however, has not been tamed by the Dharma,
So how can I give profound instructions to others?
Silly Padma Vijaya has the nature of prattling,
Like a parrot repeating OṂ MAṆI PADME HŪṂ.

So although I am unworthy and unsuitable to compose this,
The peerless lord of the family, Choktrul Rinpoche,
Placed the golden crown of command on my head.
As I was unable to refuse, I had to do as I've done.

The lotus-stem of my words and their meaning may be subtle,
But it sprouted from the pond of pure faith and samaya,
So, young bees, please land here and feast your eyes,
And don't get bogged down in the soil of criticism.

May all the goodness arising from this small collection
Of the nectar of the oral teachings of past noble beings,
Shine forth a light of lucid exposition
That opens up a hundred doorways.

By the immaculate merit arising from this,
May the lotus feet of the lord of the circle remain for long,
May the teachings flourish, the Dharma wheels of study and practice turn,
And may all beings throughout space attain supreme and complete liberation.

This text was composed by the old monk Rigdü Pemey Nyugu Tsal. Having had the great fortune of serving the two gentle protectors and vajra holders, as well as their incarnations, I wrote this while placing their lotus feet at the crown of my head. The text was composed at my home at the upper retreat of Shechen Monastery, the temple known as Dechok Tashi Gepel, and transcribed by my student, Tubten Chöpel. May this become a cause for the supreme and definitive teachings of the secret essence to remain for long.

Maṅgalaṃ. Virtue. Virtue. Virtue.

Brilliant Light

A Commentary on the Activity of Guru Vādisiṃha
That Bestows the Glory of Intelligence

Karma Rinchen Dargye

Guru Vādisiṃha (Lama Mawey Senge)

Śubhaṃ! Prajñā vardha bhavantu!

Lord of Speech of the victorious ones, Tötreng Tsal,
In the ocean of buddha fields you are one but with manifold
emanations.
In this land you are our lord, the knowledge holder Chokgyur Lingpa.
I offer my crown as an adornment to your lotus feet.

Your speech is the inexhaustible adornment wheel,
Abiding as the enjoyment body's continuous wheel of speech.
Your supreme mind of luminous great bliss is the dharma body.
Meeting you within this indivisible self-awareness, I pay homage.

Accomplishing the Guru's Mind is deeply profound and dispels all
obstacles.
It is a profound hidden treasure revealed from rock on the border
of Kham and Tibet.
It is an excellent vase of ripening and liberation,
Which you, the king of dharma, were empowered and foretold
to discover.

Upholders of the teachings, such as the twenty-five worthy ones,
And the thirty-seven masters with perfect and supreme
accomplishment,
Gurus, yidams, deities of the maṇḍala,
Ḍākinīs, and dharma protectors—please bestow auspiciousness!

Following this homage, I will now explain the stages of visualization of Guru Vādisiṃha as described in the sixth chapter of *The Essence Manual of Oral Instructions* that belongs to the cycle known as *Accomplishing the Guru's Mind: Dispeller of All Obstacles*. About this practice, the treasure text of *Condensed Activity* says:

> The essential way to accomplish this
> Is to sit on a comfortable seat in a solitary place,
> And practice the beginning, the main part, and the conclusion.

Thus, this unfailing guidance manual clearly speaks of a solitary place in the very first line. Here, however, the explanation concerns the subsequent three points: the preparation, the main part, and the conclusion.

Part 1: The Preparation

At first, you and all countless sentient beings begin by prostrating while chanting the refuge verses. In whom does one take refuge? Generally, we take refuge in the precious Three Jewels. However, in this context of secret mantra we specifically take refuge in the extraordinary objects of refuge. Here the guru is the essence of the Three Jewels, the yidam is the jewel of the Buddha, and the ḍākinīs and dharma protectors are the jewel of the Saṅgha. Moreover, the manifestation of the yidam deity as the principal figure of the maṇḍala is the Buddha. The topic, the statements of secret mantra, is the Dharma. The retinue of ḍākas and ḍākinīs are the Saṅgha. When these Three Jewels are gathered together in a single maṇḍala, they are the supreme objects of refuge. However, just knowing that your guru, the wish-fulfilling jewel, is the embodiment of the Three Jewels and the three roots will suffice. This is the intent of *The Tantra of the Emergence of Cakrasaṃvara*, which says:

> The guru is the Buddha, the guru is the Dharma.
> Likewise the guru is the Saṅgha.
> The guru is Glorious Vajradhara.

It is important to know all the causes, divisions, and trainings that pertain to this foundation stone of the general vehicle.

Generating the Twofold Mind of Awakening

Next is the generation of the twofold precious mind of awakening, the mind of awakening in aspiration and application. All our mothers, sentient beings, must be taken to the unsurpassable level of lasting happiness. However, in order for that to happen, one must first wish to attain that state. That is the mind of awakening in aspiration. Then, in order to accomplish that wish, one takes up the practice of the excellent method—the profound development and completion stages that relate to the masters of the three bodies. That is the mind of awakening in application. It is crucial to first cultivate this pure state of mind and then let it suffuse your practice.

Dispelling Obstructing Forces

Here I will explain this topic to suit an intelligent person with prior training who has confidence in the unity of the development and completion stages. This accords with the extensive practice manual for the treasure text of the *Condensed Activity*. Here, the syllables HŪṂ HRĪḤ refer to great compassion that is beyond any reference point and empty of dualistic fixation. While resting in that state, chant the verse that begins "All demons, obstructers, and evil spirits—deluded dualistic perceptions." The meaning of this verse is that, apart from the dualistic delusion of your own mind, there are no outer demons. *The Tantra of Manifest Enlightenment* says:

> There are no demons or the activity of demons.
> Like the binding of self-aware mind,
> If you tame your mind,
> All demons will be transformed!

The Magical Vajra Mirror says:

> If you abandon all thought and notions,
> There will be no activity of demons.
> Thus one is unobstructed by thoughts.
> This is taught by those who have authentic awareness.

Master Padmasambhava taught:

> When you purify the mental stains of thought and duality
> Not even the words 'obstructing force' remain.

Therefore, give a pleasant torma offering to your many thoughts—the obstructing forces of delusion—and send them off to their own abodes.

The Protection Circle

Generally, in the context of the development stage, one visualizes a vajra ground made of vajras that have blended and melded together. All directions are secured by a tall and vast circular enclosure made of upright, stacked vajras, which resembles iron mountains. There is also a vast vajra dome, in the skull-like shape of an Indian-style tent, which is attached to the fence like a lid.

On the top of the dome is a half-vajra top-ornament. At the point where the enclosure and the dome meet, on the inside is a vajra lattice, and a covering vajra canopy is spread across the meeting point. Outside of the dome there are vajra chains crossed and joined to form a vajra net, which is surrounded by thousands of pointing arrows. From the point of these arrows blaze the fires of the five wisdoms.

The upper covering supports a vajra lattice that runs along the outside. In the center of the upper covering there is a vajra top-ornament. On the exterior, the fence is bound together in its center with a vajra chain. There is also a way of explaining this in accordance with the teacher's oral instructions.

This explanation belongs to the extensive development stage. However, in accordance with the actual teaching of the *Condensed Activity* itself, one meditates on a protection boundary of suchness embraced with profound insight. This is free from any concept of subject, object, and action—like the ideas of a protector, something to protect, and the act of protecting. From *The Commentary on the Essence of Secrets*:

> The king of boundaries, nonconceptual wakefulness,
> Subdues the king of obstructing forces, conceptual thought.

The Joyous Gathering of the Eight Oral Traditions says:

> In the state where everything is bodies and wisdoms,
> There is not a single obstructing thought.
> There is no protector and nothing to be protected.

The appearance of great nondual wisdom is the deity, sound is mantra, and thoughts are the play of the dharma body; through this, the boundaries of the maṇḍala are primordially and spontaneously established. On the syllable HŪṂ, *The Vajra Peak Tantra* says:

> Whoever utters the syllable HŪṂ
> Will remove and conquer suffering.
> He will conquer the fear of existence,
> And disrupt and kill the harmful ones.
> Recall the syllable HŪṂ as supreme!

There are many ways of applying this, but here it refers to disrupting harmful beings.

VAJRA means lord of stones. The meaning of this is explained in *The Vast Magical Emanation*:

> Vajra nature conquers all obscurations
> And can be harmed by nothing.

RAKṢA RAKṢA means "Protect, protect!" BHRŪṂ embodies the five buddha families and is thus the seed syllable of the palace.

Descent of Blessings and Consecration of the Offerings

In ḍākinī language one would say HANG while in Sanskrit it is OṂ ĀḤ HŪṂ, which refers to an absence of thinking in terms of arising, dwelling, and ceasing. Moreover, OṂ is the emanation body, ĀḤ is the enjoyment body, and HŪṂ is the dharma body. In this way, these syllables signify the unborn dharma body, the unobstructed enjoyment body, and the compassionate emanation body. The first two lines of the treasure text refer to the descent of blessings, while the second two lines indicate the consecration of the offerings.

The verse for invocation begins, "Hosts of guru deities of the three bodies . . ." At this point you should recollect the dharma body—the mind lineage of the victorious ones, the enjoyment body—the symbolic lineage of the knowledge holders, and the emanation body—the human hearing lineage as well as the six treasure lineages. The lineage of empowerment by aspiration, the verbal lineage of the yellow scrolls, and the lineage of entrustment to the ḍākinīs are included in the latter, the hearing lineage of people.

When you chant the words, "manifest from space!" imagine that the host of deities belonging to the three bodies manifest. They appear from the ultimate pure realm of space within the basic space of phenomena in the form of the guru's body, speech, and mind. Imagine that they dissolve into your surroundings, which are blessed to be a pure realm; into your building, which is blessed to be a celestial palace; into your body, speech, and mind, which are blessed to become enlightened body, speech, and mind; into the offering substances and implements, such as food and drink, which are blessed as the sense pleasures of wisdom; and into the retinue, who are blessed to become gods and goddesses.

The Mantra Recitation for the Descent of Blessings

The general seed syllables for body, speech, and mind are OṂ, ĀḤ, and HŪṂ. The great knowledge holder, the lord of the treasure revealers, received a prophecy concerning the meaning of the ḍākinī mantra:

> OṂ means *ema*, amazing!
> ĀḤ means *a-le*, incredible!
> HŪṂ means *ha-ha-wa-ku*, astounding!
> Apply them in a profound manner.
> Emaho and ah-ha-ye,
> Mean *ha-ha-ma-ho*!

Vajra means lord of stones, *guru* means master, *deva* means deity, *ḍākinī* means sky traveler, *jñāna* means wisdom, and *āveśaya* means may it descend. The first of the two ĀḤ syllables indicates dissolution, while the second shows inseparability.

The line that says "All that appears and exists, manifest within the ground" refers to the following. All phenomena can be included within the twelve sense spheres, and in turn they can be further condensed into the five aggregates. The fact that these aggregates are naturally and primordially empty is the purity of the dharma body. However, their unobstructed and diverse manifestation is the emanation body. In this way, all phenomena manifest as the three bodies within the ground. Consequently, it is said that they "manifest as the ground." This is also the manner in which they are primordially pure.

Everything—the worlds and all beings—can be included in the phenomena of form, sound, smell, taste, and texture. Therefore, all of this abides within, and arises from, the ground in the form of the outer offering of the sense pleasures. Likewise, all of the inner contents—sentient beings—are made of the five nectars and also constitute the five meats, and in this way they arise from the ground as the inner offering. Moreover, all male and female beings have the nature of means and knowledge and arise from the ground as the secret offering. Likewise, all phenomena of the outer world and its inner contents are a luminous unity of means and knowledge, free from all thought constructs, and so they arise from the ground as the offering of suchness.

Beginners who have not realized phenomena to be this way should meditate by visualizing the letters RAṂ, YAṂ, and KHAṂ emerging from the three syllables that are situated in the three places. These syllables then burn, scatter, and cleanse all of the offering substances. In this way, the surrounding environment becomes a buddha field and the building one is in becomes a celestial palace.

At this point a jeweled vase emerges from the syllable BHRŪṂ, which itself is like a vessel. Within this vase is a HŪṂ syllable, which emanates offering substances and goddesses that pervade all of space. They offer cooling water, flowers, incense, light, scented water, food, and music. Now, from three ĀḤ syllables a skull container is emanated. Subsequently, the HŪṂ syllable melts within this container and turns into the nectar of the five wisdoms, which is blue, red, and pearled in color. When the ĀḤ syllable melts, it produces red rakta, which generates great bliss. As the syllable HŪṂ melts, it turns into offering tormas that goddesses of the five sense pleasures send forth. As one utters three HŪṂ syllables, all impurities in the offering articles vanish. Think that the statement OṂ SARVA PŪJĀ MEGHA ĀḤ HŪṂ fills all of space with outer, inner, and secret offering clouds. (*OṂ* means belonging to the offering, *SARVA* means all, *PŪJĀ* means offering, and *MEGHA* means cloud.) This was merely a brief explanation.

Part 2: The Main Part

The Three Samādhis

The samādhi of suchness is to rest in the undefiled natural state by recalling that all phenomena are primordially and naturally pure. This is emptiness free from elaboration, also known as self-arising wisdom. Since this suchness has never existed, it is not nonexistent. Moreover, since it has never been nonexistent, neither does it exist. Therefore, it has the nature of the three gates of liberation, which do not abide within the extremes of permanence or nihilism. These three gates are emptiness, lack of characteristics (inexpressibility), and wishlessness (not abiding in the realm of conditioned phenomena).

The samādhi of total illumination means to meditate, in a manner that is free from clinging, on all-pervasive illusory compassion for those beings who lack the realization of the samādhi of suchness.

The causal samādhi is to visualize the white letter HRĪḤ that represents the unity of emptiness and compassion.

These three samādhis purify the habitual tendencies toward birth, death, and the intermediate state. The samādhi of suchness (the moment of dissolving into luminosity during full attainment) purifies death and brings the dharma body onto the path. The samādhi of total illumination (the mental body of the intermediate state) purifies the intermediate state and brings the enjoyment body onto the path. The causal samādhi, together with the seed maṇḍala, purifies birth and becoming. (As it completely purifies the tendency toward taking future rebirths, the mind in the intermediate state becomes capable of intentionally taking one of the four types of birth.) The causal samādhi also purifies ordinary activity and brings the emanation body and its enlightened activity onto the path.

Within the vast open space of the protection circle that you previously visualized rests the syllable of the causal samādhi. This syllable gradually emanates the seed syllables for the five elements along with Mount Meru. First it projects the syllable E, which itself becomes the dark blue expansive source of phenomena, with the peak pointing downward and the wide opening pointed upward. On top of the source of phenomena appears a YAṂ syllable. This syllable becomes the maṇḍala of wind, which has the shape of a cross, encircled by dark green light. On top of the wind element, the syllable RAṂ is projected, which transforms into a maṇḍala of fire. It is triangular in shape, red in color, and encircled by swirling flames. On top of the fire element appears the syllable BAṂ, which transforms into a maṇḍala of water that is spherical, white, and encircled by white light. On top of the water element, the syllable LAṂ is projected. It transforms into the maṇḍala of earth, which is square, golden, and surrounded by yellow light. Finally, upon the earth element, from the letter SUṂ, the square-based Mount Meru emerges, made of jewels. There is also a condensed form of practice in which one simply visualizes the layered elements without having them first emerge from seed syllables.

The Celestial Palace

Above this visualized environment rests the syllable HRĪḤ of the causal samādhi. This syllable now projects a five-colored BHRŪṂ syllable, which in turn descends on the summit of Mount Meru. As this letter dissolves into light, it gives rise to the celestial palace. This way of visualizing the elements and Mount Meru within the protection circle follows the description given in *The Secret Essence of Vajrasattva* from *The New Treasures of Chokgyur Lingpa* as well as the instructions of the early knowledge holders. The meaning here, which accords with the treasure text, is that the protection circle rests *upon* the gradually stacked elements and Mount Meru. The original protection circle that was visualized previously was dissolved into emptiness during the causal samādhi when light rays radiated forth from the letter HRĪḤ and purified grasping to the reality of the world and its contents. According to our tradition, this is the way it should be visualized. There were, however, some past knowledge holders who explained that the original protection circle remains. According to this explanation, at the top of Mount Meru one visualizes a vajra ground, which is surrounded by a vajra wall, like a ring of iron mountains, blazing with five-colored fire.

Both of these traditions explain that, for wrathful retinues, the vajra ground within the vajra wall contains eight major charnel grounds. However, as Mañjuśrī is a peaceful deity they are not needed here. Buddhaguhya's *The Meaning of Maṇḍalas* says,

> The charnel ground of the wrathful ones
> Is an eternal pure realm, yet saṃsāra is not abandoned.

Within the vajra wall is a thousand-petaled lotus made of precious gems and upon its anthers is a beautiful pure realm. In the center of a double vajra is a white (or blue) square, which is twelve times as wide as it is high. The twelve prongs on the double vajra are blue on the east side, yellow in the south, red in the west, and green on the north side. The celestial palace is square and its five walls are made of five types of jewels. The jewels of the inner wall are the color of the main deity's family. Some texts teach that the five layers of walls proceeding outward from this center are colored according to the central color.

However, in this context Padmasambhava explains that one should "visualize the colors of the four activities separately." This means that the colors of the outer walls of the palace should be colored in a clockwise pattern, like it is described in *The Vajra Garland*. Accordingly, the eastern wall is blue on the outside, then green, red, and finally yellow. The southern wall is yellow on the outside, then blue, green, and red. The western side is first red, then yellow, blue, and green. Finally, the northern side is green on the outside, then red, yellow, and blue. In the center of all of this is the lord of the maṇḍala. Here, the color of the inner wall is white. (The color of the inner wall is determined by the deity's buddha family rather than the order of the colors. Therefore, instead of being red, it is white in agreement with the main text of Vādisiṃha.)

From the edge of the outer foundation protrudes a ledge of red gems. Surrounding the platform on this ledge are offering goddesses who face inward while presenting offerings. This is described in *The Meaning of Maṇḍalas*:

> All natural enjoyments,
> Beautiful forms, sweet sounds, and sumptuous scents,
> Delicious tastes, and pleasant objects
> Are joyously offered by the offering goddesses on the ledge.

At the top of the walls runs a yellow border studded lightly with jewels, like frost. On top of that are some posts, or small pillars, that together with their capital are two and a half measures high. These support a golden beam that is half a measure high and equally wide. The beam runs alongside the exterior of the layered walls and is supported by short pillars. Sometimes it is said that there are sixteen of these pillars, but here their number is not explicit. The pillars have nails about half a measure in length protruding from their four lower levels, and they are tied with golden threads. These threads are bound and tied together and are known as the "four golden belts." These four great belts are merely a method for preventing entry through the lattice. The master Buddhaguhya has explained about the place where the lattice and the tassels are attached:

> The ornamentation at the tip of the rafters is a dragonhead. From its mouth comes a garland of gems. This becomes the lattice and tassels.

As is said here, on the tip of the rafters below the ceiling there are dragons with lattices hanging from their mouths. In the center of the dragons' mouths hang bells, yak tails, and half moons, and these are the tassels. On top of the rafters is the roof, which goes out as far as the protruding foundation. Under the roof are some rainspout vessels. They are made of white gems, turned upside down and arranged like a garland. On top of the roof are jeweled boards, surmounted by a ledge that is made of three to four white boards. There are other names for this ledge depending on the context.

Inside the palace there are eight pillars that support four interlocked beams, on top of which twenty-eight rafters are fastened. Except for the skylight in the center, jeweled boards cover the ceiling so that this entire level is covered with jewels. That which we call the central chamber is made of wooden pillars, placed at each of the four corners of the skylight. Buddhaguhya also mentions the support of the roof:

> The interior eight pillars
> Support four great upper beams.
> The space between the four beams
> Is covered by twenty-eight rafters.

In this way, the ceiling covers the palace. Moreover, it is explained that the summit of the roof is a jewel that is ornamented by the sign of the buddha family. *The Great Play of Illusion* says:

> The crowning jewel blazes,
> Ornamented with the sign of the family.

In general, Guru Vādisiṃha belongs to the family of Mañjuśrī. However, in this case the deity arises in the form of the guru and, since this is more significant, he belongs to the Lotus family. Accordingly, beautiful jewels and lotus flowers adorn the summit of the palace. If you wonder whether the deity has assumed the form of the guru, he certainly has. In fact, all buddhas and bodhisattvas of the ten directions take the form of the vajra master in order to assist sentient beings. *The Sūtra of the Play of the Rainstorm* speaks of this by saying "with the intent to benefit sentient beings, I take the form of the vajra master."

In the exact center of the walls, aligned with the four cardinal directions, are four gates, each with a vestibule. The two lower corners of the vestibule meet with the protruding foundation. Four pillars support the top of each vestibule, which consists of four beams, surmounted by the levels of the eightfold architrave. These are the horse ankle, lotus, casket, lattice, cluster ornament, garlands, rainspout, and roof. The horse ankle is a blue background with a row of golden vajras arranged against it. The lotus consists of lotus petals made from red jewels. The casket is a flat box inserted in between the short pillars. The lattice is a pattern of white jewels. The cluster ornament is yellow and ornamented by fine jewels. The garland is a jeweled lattice and tassels. The rainspouts are white and look like an upside-down anointing vase. The roof is dark blue and upraised. In its center is an upright yellow wheel flanked by a male and female deer. At the very top, a white parasol adorns it all.

When training in this way, it is important to recall the purity of each and every object because otherwise one's meditation will become one-sided. Therefore, the recollection of the purity is taught as a way to train in perceiving the symbolism of the celestial palace and the bodies of the deities. This form of training is intended for those of lesser capacity who have not yet realized the natural state as it is. As such it is an illustration or a symbol of complete purification that embodies the inconceivable great compassion and activity of the buddhas.

Each of these symbolic forms points to a meaning that one should bring to mind. As for the purity of the celestial palace, the square shape represents the completely unspoiled basic space of phenomena. The four doors represent the palace of great bliss that derives from the four immeasurable contemplations. The eightfold architrave represents a complete progression through the eight vehicles so that one arrives at the practice of this nondual vehicle.

The four resultant architraves represent the four means of magnetizing. Each of these has eight streamers, which indicate the perfect qualities of the philosophical systems found in the eight vehicles. The maṇḍala itself represents the unbroken continuity of turning the wheel of dharma. The protruding foundation represents the four applications of mindfulness. The pillars of the architraves represent the four authentic eliminations. The four vestibules represent the four bases of miraculous abilities. The five layers of the wall represent the five faculties. The borders, top borders, rainspouts, ledges, and the chamber represent the five powers. The various ornaments—the jeweled latticework, the ornamented tassels, the flower garland, silk streamers, mirrors, the form of the moon, and the tail fan—represent the seven aspects of enlightenment. The eight pillars represent the eightfold noble path. The pillar capitals are the eight liberations. The four beams are the four fearlessnesses.

The twenty-eight inner small beams represent the eighteen types of emptiness and the ten perfections. The arrangement of the ceiling symbolizes inconceivable qualities. The four supportive nails represent the four authentic reasonings. The top ornament represents the fact that all of the Buddha's maṇḍalas are within the expanse of awareness wisdom. The parasols in the four corners indicate that all beings are protected with great compassion. Similarly, the seats represent great compassion.

The light rays shining in all directions represent the constantly clear and shining eternal wheel of adornment that is the enlightened body, speech, and mind. The all-pervasive and unobscured vibrant clarity indicates that everything is exclusively an expression of wisdom. The base of the double vajras represents the wisdom of emptiness. The twelve spokes represent the purification of the twelve links of dependent origination. The lotuses represent the inherent nature, which is free from any stain. The eight charnel grounds represent the natural purity of the eight collections of consciousness and indicate the eight examples of the illusory nature of phenomena. The spokes in the vajra represent nonconceptual wisdom. The pits of fire represent the fire of wisdom burning up demons and negative emotions.

It is very important to recall the purity of the various aspects in this way. As a beginner you may be unable to recall the purity of all of the elements at once. In that case you can simply recall that all the parts of the palace arise as a symbolic indication of all the Buddha's inconceivable qualities of abandonment and realization. If you can think in this way, it will be an approximation of the recollection of purity.

The Seat and the Deities

The Essence Manual of Oral Instructions says:

> On the anthers of a multicolored lotus, upon a sun and
> moon disc.

Accordingly, here one should visualize a multicolored lotus with eight petals, placed in the center of the celestial palace. On its pistils and anthers rests another multicolored lotus, above which is a sun disc and a moon disc. In each of the eight cardinal and intermediate directions, are eight additional lotus seats. Finally, on top of the sun and moon discs of the central lotus rests a white syllable HRĪḤ.

As this syllable transforms, it becomes Guru Vādisiṃha. His appearance is that of a paṇḍita, with a whitish complexion tinged with red and radiant like the moon. He is loving like a mother and unrivalled in his splendor. He possesses all of the major and minor marks. His two hands are at his heart center, held one above the other in the gesture of teaching the dharma. With joined thumb and index fingers at his heart center, he holds two lotus stems with petals that bloom next to his ears. The lotus at his right ear holds a copy of *The Perfection of Wisdom in Eight Thousand Verses*, which embodies the three collections. The lotus at his left ear supports a volume of Vajrakīlaya teachings belonging to the vehicle of secret mantra, namely *The Vidyottama Tantra: The Vajrakīlaya Tantra That Fulfills All Wishes*.

The practice manual says that he is "in the dress of a paṇḍita," which means that he wears the monastic lower robe, a stitched lower robe, a shawl, a reddish shawl with golden stitches, another reddish shawl with golden stitches and designs, and a paṇḍita's short-sleeved shirt that is blue at the border of the upper arms. He looks beautiful wearing his red paṇḍita hat, known as "the jeweled diadem," that covers his crown protuberance and his diadem. Visualize him clearly as someone who fully embodies the combined intelligence of all buddhas and bodhisattvas in the ten directions.

Around Guru Vādisiṃha, on each of the eight lotus petals there are individual lotus seats. On the eastern lotus sits the radiant white Mañjuśrīvīra. His right hand is in the offering gesture and his left, placed at his heart, is in the gesture of teaching the dharma while holding the stems of two lotuses that bloom by his ears. The lotuses support a sword and a volume of scripture. To the south is the orange Mañjuśrī Vāgīśvara. His hands are at his heart center in the gesture of turning the wheel of dharma while holding the stems of two utpala flowers that bloom by his ears. The flowers support a sword and a volume of scripture. In the west is Mañjuśrī Vādirāṭ, who is red in color. His two hands rest in the gesture of equanimity and hold lotuses that support a sword and a volume of scripture. In the north is Mañjuśrī Vajratīkṣṇa, who is dark blue and looks slightly wrathful. In his right hand he brandishes an upraised sword, and his left hand, at his heart center in the dharma-teaching gesture, holds a lotus, upon which rests a volume of scripture. All four are seated in the vajra posture.

In the southeast is white Vajra Sarasvatī, in the southwest is yellow Jewel Sarasvatī, in the northwest is red Lotus Sarasvatī, and in the northeast is green Action Sarasvatī. All four wear silk garments and jeweled ornaments and sit cross-legged with their knees upraised. Each one holds in her left hand a jeweled lute of the same color as her body, which she plays with the fingers of her right hand. All the Mañjuśrīs of the four families and the four consorts are adorned with the thirteen types of enjoyment body ornaments, and they face the main deity. At the four doors, facing outward, stand the four great kings, dressed like gods. To the east is white Dhṛitaraśṭaḥ, who holds a lute. To the south is the dark blue Virudhaka, holding a sword. To the west is red Virūpakasa, who holds a stūpa and a snake lasso. To the north is yellow Vaiśravaṇa, holding a victory banner and a mongoose. Visualize that in the space between all of this, filling the space like cloudbanks, are manifestations of the guru who is the root of all blessings, the yidam who is the root of accomplishment, and the ḍākinīs and dharma protectors who are the root of enlightened activity.

Recollecting Purity

The Purity of Guru Vādisiṃha

Guru Vādisiṃha's single face indicates the single essence of the dharma body. His two hands indicate the method of great compassion and the wisdom of emptiness. Since saṃsāra and nirvāṇa are equal and because he does not abide in either of those extremes, his two legs are crossed in the vajra posture. In accordance with his outward discipline, he wears the robes of a fully ordained monk. Because of his inward practice of secret mantra, he wears a diadem. Their unity is shown as he takes the form of a vajra master who wears a paṇḍita hat. Since the real aspect, the dharma body, arises as the enjoyment body, he has all the major and minor marks, and his plaited hair is bound in a topknot and ornamented with a diadem. As he accepts ordinary disciples, he appears as a supreme emanation body in monastic robes. He wears the red paṇḍita hat because he has manifested in the form of the vajra master, who is lord of the maṇḍala. Vimalamitra's *Secret Path of Wisdom* mentions this hat in the following way:

> He wears a hat with a pen-tip representing the highest view,
> That outshines other views and overcomes opposing arguments.
> On the hat the flaps of compassion hang down.
> Its color is that of dominion over saṃsāra and nirvāṇa.

The "pen-tipped hat" refers to the red paṇḍita hat. It has a spherical shape that resembles a flax fruit with flaps hanging down. It is said that Ratna Lingpa once had a vision in which the earflaps of the hat touched the ground. Moreover, at Samye Monastery is the image of Padmasambhava that he felt resembled himself. This statue wears a hat that represents the teaching of the three collections. It is similar to Guru Vādisiṃha's hat except that its flaps look like a lion's nose. Therefore, the former hat with the long earflaps is the one that the great paṇḍita Guru Vādisiṃha wears, while the latter is like the one worn by Kyechok Tsulsang.

In Guru Vādisiṃha's right hand is the volume of wisdom resting on the lotus of skillful means. The text that he holds is *The Perfection of Wisdom in Eight Thousand Verses*, which embodies the entire meaning of all the general teachings. This sūtra teaching points directly at emptiness and explains the perfection of wisdom. It is therefore the ultimate teaching that reveals how all phenomena, from form up to and including omniscience, are emptiness. However, since the realization of emptiness depends on a method and can be resolved only by relying on such, he also holds the lotus of method in his right hand.

In his left hand he holds a tantric volume of secret mantra, which shows the method of great bliss. The meaning of this method can be realized only through the touch of the wisdom lotus, and to indicate this he also holds a thousand-petaled lotus. When Padmasambhava was practicing at Yangleshö in Nepal, he was able to fully realize the level of a knowledge holder of the great seal without any obstacles due to his practice of Vajrakīlaya. For that reason, Guru Vādisiṃha holds a volume of that tantra in his left hand as a symbol of wisdom. Moreover, as a symbol that Guru Vādisiṃha turns the wheel of dharma of the vast and profound unity of sūtra and mantra—method and wisdom—he holds the two lotuses in the gesture of turning the wheel of dharma.

Additionally, in more detail, the six aspects of means and wisdom—his two hands, two lotuses, and two volumes of scripture—symbolize the path of the six perfections. This correlates in the following way. The right volume of scripture represents wisdom, the right lotus generosity, and his right hand discipline. The left volume of scripture represents diligence, the left lotus meditative concentration, and his left hand patience. To reach the perfection of wisdom one must rely on generosity and the other methods and, moreover, in order to prevent virtues, such as generosity, from being exhausted one must be disciplined. Therefore, in order to practice the development and completion stages of the profound secret mantra, one must be fiercely diligent and patiently uphold the meaning of the profound secret mantra. Generosity, discipline, and diligence pertain to the aspect of method, while the perfection of wisdom, meditative concentration, and patience pertain to the aspect of knowledge. Additionally, it is said that patience and diligence accompany the other four. In this way, there are many ways to explain this topic. However, here I have explained it mostly as it applies to purity. I have refrained from citing texts to support these points out of the concern that I would end up writing too much!

Guru Vādisiṃha's white color indicates the stainless dharma body, while the reddish tinge of his skin shows his compassion and affection for sentient beings. Since he is adorned with the nine traits of peaceful demeanor, there is nothing unsettling about him, and he appears wholly appealing. These nine traits can be explained differently according to the ancient tradition of Zur and the teachings of Longchen Rabjam. Here I will explain them following Longchenpa:

1. His body is soft and attractive to indicate the purification of birth.
2. The three parts of his body are well proportioned since sickness is purified.

3. His body is not loose but remains firm to show the purification of death.
4. His back is like a fir tree, the metaphor for straightness.
5. His beautiful body is soft and youthful since he has purified old age.

These are the five essential qualities. Then follow the remaining four:

6. He is clean, resplendent, and bedecked with the flowers of the major marks and the fruits of the minor marks.
7. His body is dazzling and lustrous since he has perfected the sphere of totality.
8. He is magnificent and stunningly beautiful.
9. His overwhelming splendor captivates his disciples.

Guru Vādisiṃha is also endowed with the thirty-two major marks of a buddha in the following way:

1. On the palms and soles of his feet are thousand-spoked wheels that shine brilliantly as if carved into ivory.
2. The soles of his feet settle evenly upon the ground like a mirror or a turtle's belly.
3. His fingers are webbed like the swan, the king of birds.
4. His hands and feet are smooth like the petals of a lotus or the extremely youthful and firm skin of a newborn baby.
5. He has seven parts that are rounded: the hollows of his collar bones, the principal hollows of the thumbs and big toes of his hands and feet, and the hollow at the nape of his neck.
6. His fingers are long and magnificently slender.
7. His wide heels protrude outward a quarter of the length of his feet.
8. Because he is four times larger than ordinary beings, his body is large and straight, without any crookedness.
9. The protuberance on the outside of his ankle bones is not visible.

10. All of the hairs on his body point upward.
11. His calves are well proportioned, being expansive and curved in all the right places like those of the enaya animal. Lord Mikyo Dorje explains that this is a deer, while the Master Dharmamitra mentions that it is an eight-legged lion.
12. His long and beautiful arms extend to his knees.
13. His genitals are not visible as they are withdrawn into a sheath like an elephant's or a stallion's.
14. He is radiant and pure like the finest gold.
15. His skin is free from wrinkles, sagging, or shriveling. As such it is firm, even, and smooth.
16. Each of his hairs is fine and radiant and curls to the right.
17. He has a fine and soft hair tuft between his eyes that is very white and glistening and curls naturally to the right.
18. His upper body is broad and expansive like a lion, the king of animals.
19. His two upper arms are well rounded.
20. His two shoulder blades do not have depressions.
21. His tongue is not blemished with wind, bile, or phlegm, and so even unpleasant tastes are delicious.
22. He is vast and uniform like the bodhi tree.
23. His crown protuberance measures four of his own fingers and protrudes upward from the top of his head, but is invisible to gods and men.
24. His tongue is long and beautiful, and if extended, it reaches his hairline and the hollow of his ears.
25. He has mastery over the speech of Brahma endowed with sixty aspects.
26. His cheeks are rounded like a mirror and broad like a lion's jowls.
27. His teeth are extremely white, never tarnished by stains or food.
28. His teeth are equal in size and length.
29. He never has to chew more than twice, even if the food is very tough, and because his teeth are without gaps, they do not shift.

30. He has more teeth than ordinary people who have twenty-eight or thirty-two. Including the four canines, he has forty teeth.
31. His eyes are the color of a deep radiant sapphire, and all parts are perfectly delineated and completely free from redness.
32. His eyelashes are glossy and deep black, like those of a supreme bull. (According to *Endowed with Purity* they are like that of a cow, an elephant, or a supreme bull. *The Supreme Essence* and *The Ornament of Realization* describe them like those of a calf.)

Likewise, the eighty minor marks are also present on Guru Vādisiṃha's body in the following manner, listed in eight sets of ten:

(1) His nails are copper colored and (2) glossy since he is healthy and nourished. (3) Since he is from an aristocratic family, the nails are also long and fine. (4) Moreover, his nails are rounded, (5) broad, and (6) tapered. (7) The veins are not visible and (8) are free from knots. (9) The inner ankle bones are not apparent, and (10) his feet are equal in size so that one is not longer than the other. This is the first group of ten marks.

(1) He walks with a lion's gait to captivate humans. (2) He moves with an elephant's gait to humble the nāgās. (3) He moves like a swan through space. (4) As the leader of all beings, he moves like a supreme garuda bird. (5) When passing someone, he keeps that person to his right as a sign that others are more important. (6) Skilled in beauty, he walks elegantly. (7) He is never deceitful and therefore walks unwaveringly. (8) His skin is never loose and always supple, full, and beautiful. (9) His body always appears as if it has just been washed. (10) His body parts are excellently proportioned. This is the second group of ten marks.

(1) His body is perfectly clean, (2) smooth, (3) pure, and (4) possesses all of the major marks. (5) The trunk of his body is broad, and his body and limbs are large. (6) He walks with even steps. (7) His eyes are very clear. (8) His body is extremely firm and youthful. (9) His flesh is

never slack. (10) His body is robust, without any sunken places. This is the third group of ten marks.

(1) His body is excellently firm, and he is strong and very fast. (2) His limbs are very beautiful and well proportioned. (3) His vision is excellent, with no eye problems. (4) His hips are round. (5) His waistline is well shaped. (6) His belly is not sunken. (7) The face of his navel is precipitous, while his belly is flat. (8) He has a deep navel, (9) the interior of which swirls to the right. (10) All of the parts of his body are beautiful to see, and in this way, he is very attractive. This is the fourth group of ten marks.

(1) His conduct is always excellent. (2) He has no moles on his body. (3) His hands are extremely soft, like cotton. (4) The lines on his hands glow and emanate light. (5) The lines on his hands are deep set. (6) The lines on his hands are long. (7) His lips are not too long. (8) His lips, like a fruit, are red and shining. (9) His tongue is very strong and (10) slender. This is the fifth group of ten marks.

(1) His tongue is red, and (2) his speech is like thunder, (3) yet melodious and pleasant sounding. (4) His four canine teeth are round, (5) sharp, (6) white, (7) even, and (8) tapered. (9) The ridge of his nose is high. (10) The inside of his nose is clean. This is the sixth group of ten marks.

(1) His large eyes are oblong, and (2) his eyelashes are thick. (3) The shape of his eyes is like a lotus petal. (4) His eyebrows are long, (5) soft, (6) glossy, and (7) the hairs are the same length. (8) His arms are long and broad. (9) His earlobes are long and even. (10) His hearing is excellent, and his ears are evenly placed. This is the seventh group of ten marks.

(1) His forehead is well proportioned and beautiful (2) as well as broad. (3) His head is broad like a parasol. (4) His hair is black like a bee or a black flower, (5) fairly thick, (6) smooth and fine, (7) untangled, (8) does not stray upward and is not rough. (9) Moreover, it is perfumed and enchanting. (10) The endless knot marks his heart center, and auspicious signs adorn his arms and legs. This is the eighth group of ten marks, concluding the eighty marks.

Although a universal emperor is also adorned with the major and minor marks, the wheels on his hands and feet do not have a rim, and are therefore more like weapon wheels; they are also rather unclear. Self-realized buddhas also have marks, such as a crooked crown protuberance, but these are merely similar to a buddha's marks. In particular, only a buddha speaks with sixty melodious aspects, has an unapparent straight and noble crown protuberance that resembles a noble tree, perfect radiance, and a circle of hair between his eyebrows like a full moon.

The Purity of the Surrounding Deities

As a sign that they are genuinely free from the torment of negative emotions, they wear a white upper garment of silk with golden designs, a skirt, and multicolored streamers as adornments. To symbolize that they have truly mastered the virtuous teaching, their plaited hair is gathered into a top-knot. Since they do not abandon sense pleasures but enjoy them as an ornament of wisdom, they are adorned with the eight precious jewels and flowers. The sword cuts through the web of ignorance, and the volume of scripture explains all there is to know. As a symbol that sound is empty and free from arising and ceasing and able to clear away all troubles of existence and peace, the consorts play a lute that calls out the melodious sounds of dharma.

The colors of the four families of Mañjuśrī also have meaning. White symbolizes stainless wisdom. Orange indicates the blossoming of wisdom. Red symbolizes that sentient beings are attracted through the four means of magnetizing. Green shows that the four activities are spontaneously accomplished.

Additional Characteristics

The lion is the king of all animals, and in the same way, Guru Vādisiṃha is fearless among teachers of the four truths of the noble ones since he expounds the teaching of the great vehicle. Thus he is the Lion of Speech, free from unruly emotions. Tender with great love and gentle behavior, he is a protector of all beings. In essence, he is a hero who has conquered the four demons by manifesting as a deity out of mirrorlike wisdom—the complete purification of anger.

The four demons are the demon of the divine child, the demon of the lord of death, the demon of the aggregates, and the demon of negative emotions. The demon of the divine child refers to those who are like the evil lord of the gods that enjoy the emanations of others. It fully manifests in the nonvirtuous minds of sentient beings. According to the general meaning, the demon of the lord of death is the Lord of Dharma, Yamarāja, who lives on the southern horizon and controls the lifespan and vitality of sentient beings. He is mentioned in scriptures such as *The Sūtra on the Application of Mindfulness* and *Realization of the Eight Accounts of Yamāntaka*.

However, in accordance with the definitive meaning of the Buddha's most essential teaching, phenomena are not created by someone who subsequently controls them. Instead, the demon of the lord of death is understood as the fear that is present within an individual person's mind.

The demon of the aggregates refers to the assembled constituents that appear as a body due to the power of karma. The demon of the divine child refers to all distraction and deception that is based on ego clinging. The demon of negative emotions consists of all root and subsidiary negative emotions. It can, however, also be understood as simply the three poisons. When a person acts on these emotions, this gives rise to the aggregates. Therefore, according to the vehicle of the perfections, one can successively conquer the other three demons by destroying their cause, the demon of negative emotions. However, here in the great tradition of the unsurpassable vehicle of mantra, the four "causal and resultant demons" are conquered simultaneously so that they need not be averted ever again. This is explained in scriptures such as *The Sūtra of the Deeply Wrathful Compassion of the Hero Mañjuśrī*.

Guru Vādisiṃha has mastered the speech of the victorious ones, and therefore he is also known as Vāgīśvara, the Lord of Speech, who essentially is the wisdom of equanimity—the natural purity of pride. As the vajra speech of the victorious ones, he is also known as Vādirāṭ, the

Ruler of Speech. In this form his essence is discerning wisdom—the natural purity of desire. Finally, as he destroys the mountains of wrong views and cuts the net of misunderstanding, he is known as Vajratīkṣṇa, the Sharp Vajra. This is the form of all-accomplishing wisdom—the natural purity of jealousy.

As for the four families of Sarasvatī, Vajra Sarasvatī subdues all negative emotions. Jewel Sarasvatī acquires all that is needed and desired. Lotus Sarasvatī magnetizes, being attractive in all ways. Finally, Action Sarasvatī unobstructedly accomplishes the benefit of all sentient beings. They are called Sarasvatī, meaning the Melodious One, because their nature is the melody of the three realms and in actuality they are born from the melodious speech of all the victorious ones.

Lastly, the entire retinue and the celestial palace should be viewed exclusively as manifestations of empty superior wisdom, which otherwise lack reality. They appear like rainbows in the sky or like planets and stars reflected in a clear lake—apparent yet unreal. So one should make sure to rest by recollecting how all phenomena appear in mutual dependency. First, however, one should just concentrate on visualizing the deity. Then, subsequently one should contemplate how this amazing method conveys the buddhas' inconceivable qualities, the wisdom of the dharma body, their immeasurable compassion, and their enlightened activity. By doing that and resting with one-pointed devotion, one will be approximating the recollection of purity, so this is also an important point.

Blessings and Empowerment

Master Buddhaguhya's *Stages of the Path* teaches:

> In the three places—the forehead, throat, and heart center—
> Meditate on the blessing of the three vajras.
> At the five places on the head are the five wisdoms.
> One is adorned with the complete empowerment of the five wisdoms.

Accordingly, make the five-pronged vajra gesture at your forehead and utter the syllable OṂ. At the same time, visualize that inside the bone mansion of your brain is a white OṂ syllable that rests on a moon disc, clear and blazing. This represents the vajra body. Then make the three-pointed vajra gesture at your throat and utter the syllable ĀḤ. At this point you should visualize an eight-petaled red lotus at your throat. In the center of the lotus is the red syllable ĀḤ, clear and blazing. This represents vajra speech. Lastly, make the one-pointed vajra gesture at your heart center and utter the syllable HŪṂ. Now visualize a sun disc at your heart center upon which is a deep blue HŪṂ syllable, clear and blazing. This represents the vajra mind.

On some occasions one visualizes the three deities of body, speech, and mind at these points. Here, however, it is fine not to visualize the forms of deities with hands, faces, and so forth. This is due to the power of visualizing the syllables, which themselves are the form of wisdom, and because the three vajras are the nature of the five wisdoms.

When bestowing the empowerment of the five wisdom families, you should utter the syllables OṂ HŪṂ TRAṂ HRĪḤ ĀḤ and, for ease of recitation, you can keep the syllables in their usual order. However, for the gestures and the visualization, you should do it in the following way. First, extend your middle fingers and hold your hands at the back of your head and say OṂ. Then, extend your index fingers, hold your hands at your forehead and say HŪṂ. Now, extend your ring fingers, hold your hands behind your right ear and say TRAṂ. Then, extend your thumbs, holding your hands on top of your head and say HRĪḤ. Finally, extend your little fingers, hold your hands behind your left ear and say ĀḤ. Visualize that each of the seed syllables, which are the essence of the five families, rest on moon discs within the jeweled crown. At this point you should say ABHIṢIÑCA, which means that the empowerment is actually bestowed. The explanatory tantra, *The Vajra Peak*, speaks of the syllable HŪṂ in the following way:

> HŪṂ is enlightened body, speech, and mind.
> It brings about attainment of the vajra mind.

Invite the wisdom beings, dissolve them into one, and request them to remain in the following manner. As the samaya being, you first project a HŪṂ syllable from your heart center. This syllable projects light rays in the shape of hooks that naturally and spontaneously pervade countless buddha-fields, such as the Copper-Colored Mountain and the celestial palace of Lotus Light. Imagine that this light causes all the thus-gone ones of the ten directions and four times to arise from the dharma body in the form of emanation bodies. They arise in exactly the same form that you, the samaya being, have assumed, and then they arrive where you are. As *The Galtreng* says:

> Having manifested oneself as the great maṇḍala,
> Even without visualizing the invitation and request,
> One can attain the bodies and wisdoms
> Of the deities in the naturally established maṇḍala
> By summoning them with SAMĀJAḤ and E HI.

As you chant the syllables HŪṂ HRĪḤ, they invoke the samaya beings and the wisdom beings. Then recite the following verse for the invitation:

> From the supreme emanated celestial realm . . .

Thus, melodiously and with deep devotion, invite the knowledge holder guru along with the infinite ocean of the three roots from the pure realm of the Lotus Net on the glorious mountain in the southwestern continent of Cāmara. As you do so, the guru will come due to his immeasurable great compassion that is committed to liberate beings. Request him to dispel all obstacles, such as the outer obstacles of the four elements, the inner obstacles of the channels and energies, and the secret obstacles of deluded thought. Then, supplicate him to bestow the supreme and common accomplishments and recite the mantra for the invitation.

The meaning of this mantra is as follows:

The three syllables are indivisible from the three bodies.
The lord of the family of the vajra guru
Manifests the circle of the lotus maṇḍala.

Moreover, Tötreng Tsal (Powerful Skull Garland) is his secret name in Tibetan. It was given to him because he is the Skull-Adorned Buddha. According to *The Eight Teachings of Great Accomplishment*, he is the sovereign of all maṇḍalas, as it says, "Buddha Thöpa Tsal is the Lord of the family." VAJRA SAMAYA DZAḤ means, "remember your vajra commitment and come!" SIDDHI PHALA HŪṂ means, "grant excellent spiritual accomplishments and dissolve into me in a lasting manner." Then, imagine that the natural wisdom maṇḍala dissolves into the samaya maṇḍala just like water being poured into water and the two become of the same taste, completely indivisible. DZAḤ HŪṂ BAṂ HOḤ has the meaning of inciting the deities by means of the four immeasurables to accomplish the benefit of the beings. Thus, one summons the deities through compassion, binds them through love, shackles them through joy, and intoxicates them with equanimity. Additionally, *The Great Bliss Union of the Buddhas* mentions:

Invited, they enter and are bound.
When they arrive, one brings them under control.
DZAḤ HŪṂ BAṂ HOḤ
Is the sign of all of the buddhas.

Therefore, in this way the wisdom beings are summoned to the samaya beings, enter them indivisibly, and are bound in an indestructible manner until the attainment of enlightenment.

The meaning of the statement "happily take your seat" is that the deities are entreated. Moreover, the request for the deities to remain is explicitly found in both the medium-length and extensive activity liturgies in the verse that begins with "Delightful celestial palace . . ." However, here in this condensed liturgy, the request for the deities to remain takes place by reciting the mantra. Finally, regarding the last words in the mantra, SAMAYA means "sacred commitment," TIṢTHA "within the support", and LHAN "please remain."

Praise and Offerings to the Nondual Maṇḍala

The Praises

In the realm of Joyful Emanations there are gods who delight in their own emanated enjoyments. Similarly, in order to respectfully pay homage, imagine that you, as the Lord, emanate activity beings from your heart center to pay homage, like one candle lighting another. Then chant the verse:

> HŪṂ HRĪḤ Without arising, ceasing, or changing . . .

This verse praises Guru Vādisiṃha as being a wish-fulfilling jewel because he fulfills the hopes of beings through his compassionate enlightened activity. For this reason he is an object of homage for the maṇḍala deities. However, true homage is to meet him as indivisible from self-awareness. The master Nāgārjuna wrote:

> Like pouring water into water,
> Like mixing butter with butter,
> Clearly seeing your own wisdom
> Is paying homage.

However, in a mere symbolic manner, you gather the accumulations by paying homage to the excellent qualities of the deities of the maṇḍala with an extremely devoted attitude. Finally, the words ATI PŪ HOḤ are a sign of paying homage. The words PRATIŚA HOḤ signify giving a delighted reply.

The Offerings

There are four types of offering: outer, inner, secret, and the offering of suchness. First are the general outer and inner offerings.

The Outer Offerings

From the heart center of yourself as the Lord, limitless offering goddesses emanate forth and offer inconceivable clouds of outer and inner offerings that fill all realms and fields of experience. Beginning with OṂ ĀḤ HŪṂ, the syllables of the three vajras, make offerings and chant the offering verse:

> I offer the outer offerings, an ocean of sense pleasures, gathered like clouds.

Imagine that the offering goddesses offer clear and sweet water to drink and cool and pristine bathing water for refreshing the hands and feet. For the eyes they give land- and water-grown flowers of many colors, and for the nose they present delicious-smelling incense made of both natural and produced scents. For the eyes they offer the sun and the moon, jewels, and various lights, such as oil lamps. Moreover, they offer sandal- and saffron-scented bathing water for the heart center and nutritious and delicious food for the tongue. They also produce various melodious sounds for the ears, such as the sound of cymbals and various types of music that are blown, played, beaten, and strummed. At the end of the offering, the goddesses dissolve into the respective sense faculties.

The Inner Offerings

The inner offering consists of medicine, torma, and rakta.

Offering Medicine

As the essence of natural unfabricated nectar, all phenomena of saṃsāra and nirvāṇa are primordially pure. *The Tantra of Mahottara's Assembly* mentions this:

> Ego clinging purified is the body of wisdom.

Lack of attachment is the unborn basic space of phenomena.
The nondual reality arises in manifold ways.
This is the ultimate nectar.

Nectar consists of eight main ingredients that each have an outer, inner, and secret aspect. Moreover, since the five primary nectars each have these eight main ingredients, there are a total of forty divisions. Furthermore, since each of these forty divisions has twenty-five ingredients, there are one thousand different divisions. In this way, there are eight main and one thousand subsidiary ingredients to nectar.

According to Padmasambhava, the ingredients are (1) the five primary, (2) the five essential, (3) the five resultant, (4) the five qualities, (5) the five tamed, (6) the five assembled, (7) the five aims, and (8) the five useful requisites, making a total of forty ingredients. Each of these is then multiplied by twenty-five, making one thousand.

Moreover, the eight main outer ingredients are all present in the type of sandalwood known as "snake heart" in the following way. (1) Its trunk consists of dark sandalwood. (2) Its root is *mūla pattri*. (3) Its branches are clove. (4) Its leaves are crocus. (5) Its flowers are saffron. (6) Its fruits are nutmeg. (7) Its sap is camphor. (8) Its bark is cinnamon.

The eight main inner ingredients are all contained in the supreme great being. These are (1) the matrix of existence: the navel; (2) the trunk: flesh and blood; (3) the branches: the four limbs; (4) the leaves: the nails and hair; (5) the flowers: the five faculties; (6) the fruits: the five essential organs; (7) the essence: marrow, blood, brain, and spinal cord; (8) the bark: the skin.

The eight main secret ingredients are the four male buddhas, who are the four causes, and the four female buddhas, who are the four conditions. These are (1) the syllable HANG, (2) the spinal cord, (3) the fruit, (4) the pathway, which is the great channel, and (1) the bladder and liver, (2) the vessel, (3) the lotus door, and (4) the anthers. Moreover, when multiplying each of these eight main ingredients by the 125 parts, there are one thousand individual aspects.

According to the master Hūṃkāra, the eight main ingredients are the six causes together with conditions and enlightenment itself, making eight. These are (1) a master who is skilled in means, (2) his skillful consort, (3) arriving in the maṇḍala, (4) a dark brown seamless leather bowl, (5) stainless white pearls, (6) unblemished red sandalwood, (7) the medicine of the nectar of immortality, and (8) the wisdom that dispels ignorance.

The eight main ingredients mentioned by the master are: (1) view, (2) meditation, (3) conduct, (4) union, (5) liberation, (6) medicine, (7) samaya vows, and (8) empowerment.

According to master Vimalamitra, the eight main ingredients are present in the five sacred substances. Here it should be understood that each of the five substances contains the eight main ingredients. Accordingly, the eight main ingredients in the nectar of awakened mind are the eight collections of consciousness. The eight main elements of excrement are the six internal organs and the upper and lower eyes. The eight main ingredients of *maṃsa* are the calves, the upper arms, the two cheeks, and the two breasts. The eight main ingredients of rakta are the two long channels, the two great channels, the two arm channels, the heart channel, and the life-force channel. The eight main ingredients of urine are the five faculties together with body, speech, and mind. It is explained that each of these can be multiplied by twenty-five to make a total of one thousand.

When prepared in this way, this sacred substance is an elixir that causes realization of the equality of all phenomena, free from accepting and rejecting, and clears away the demon of dualistic thought. This is how the term "nectar" is explained according to the Tibetan language. However, in Sanskrit the word for nectar is *amṛta*. Here, *mṛ* means "losing the life force" while *kta* is a suffix. Then, when adding a negation particle before *mṛ*, the whole word becomes *amṛta*, which means "immortal." *The Embodiment of Realization* says:

> The vessel for nectar is a skull cup.
> The content is the streaming nectar of awakened mind.

> The condition is the ability to bring about the three results.
> The goal is immortality.
> The task is to conquer that which stains realization.
> For this reason the nectar of amṛta
> Happily fulfills the gods when they touch it.
> When it touches demons, it brings them under control.
> When it touches a practitioner, his obscurations are purified.
> When it touches an enemy, it pulverizes him.
> When it touches an obstacle maker, it intoxicates.
> When it touches a substance, it gives it strength.
> Whatever it contacts becomes powerful.

As it says here, it is necessary for the substances to be authentically blessed. These days, however, there are some "ritual specialists" who just pour a little alcohol and tea in two cups and arrogantly proclaim it to be nectar and rakta. With such substances it is difficult to fulfill the wishes of the yidam deities and to keep the protectors bound. So, failing that, how could one ever achieve what is truly meaningful, such as spiritual accomplishment and enlightened activity? Instead, one's practice simply becomes the reflection of an authentic ritual. To attract the deities and oath-bound protectors, the practitioner needs pure samaya vows and proper view and meditation. Only then will the words of the mantra and the ritual be pure and one's samādhi clear. It is therefore important to begin the ritual by gathering a complete set of substances and ritual implements and keeping them pure.

First, the base substance of the nectar is called "great heroic alcohol." It consists of a mixture of five types of alcohol made from barley, rice, wheat, grapes, and flower honey. Our supreme refuge, the great treasure revealer, directly added the dharma medicine of accomplishment to the eight main outer ingredients. The inner and secret main ingredients are the dharma medicine of the accomplishment of the great knowledge holder masters of the past. This includes the great knowledge holders from India, such as Prahevajra, Śri Siṃha, Vimalamitra, and Padmasambhava, as well as the twenty-five, or sometimes one thousand, accomplished masters from Tibet, such as Namkey Nyingpo, Vairocana, Jñānakumāra, and Sangye Yeshe. The dharma medicine of all these masters is actually present in the revealed treasures.

These blessed sacred substances also contain substances such as the red and white nectars of awakened mind of the guru and his consort, the flesh of someone born a Brahmin seven times, as well as the flesh, brain, blood, bones, excrement, and urine of many undeniably noble beings. For this reason, it is not necessary to additionally add the five nectars of an ordinary being. This dharma medicine amṛta should then be added to clean alcohol from an unopened container or to clean water. Alternatively, for the sake of convenience, it is also permissible to mix it with melted butter.

Cleanliness is of extreme importance because, although the wisdom deities have no such concept, the attendant oath-bound dharma protectors will angrily deliver punishment if any of the samaya substances and offering tormas are soiled or dirty. That is why I have elaborated here on the importance of gathering all the sacred substances and keeping them clean.

In the context of the extensive practice manual, one should first perform the blessing of the substances as the essence of the five wisdoms and the five buddha families. Following that, the recitation of the names from the offering of medicine should be inserted. At the same time, visualize that you stir the ocean of nectar with the sun and moon sphere of the thumb and ring finger and then scatter the nectar. In any case, imagine that the host of nectar deities are satisfied with the taste of great bliss.

Offering the Torma

Visualize the torma plate, which is as vast and open as the basic space of phenomena. On this plate is the sacred substance, the marvelous torma. It appears in the form of food and drinks, the five sense pleasures, and countless enjoyments. In essence, however, it is wisdom nectar. Alternatively, it is also suitable to visualize the torma as having been emanated by the goddesses of sense pleasure.

Offering Rakta

The root of suffering, in the form of subtle attachment, converges and dissolves into the expanse of great bliss free from attachment. This is offered to the host of maṇḍala deities of the great sacred substance that liberates cyclic existence into basic unborn space.

This offering substance can be described in terms of its essence, etymology, and its divisions. The essence of the basic rakta of existence is the element of water. The essence of the apparent, symbolic rakta is the pure color red. The essence of the unchanging, true rakta is the purity of desire, which is the identity of discriminating wisdom, Amitāyus. The essence of the saṃsāric, causal rakta is human rakta, the blood of the womb. The essence of the resultant rakta of great bliss is the heart blood from the liberation of evil Rudra.

The meaning of the word "rakta" is as follows. When speaking of the color, "rakta" means red. In the context of activity, it means desire. In terms of an actual object, it refers to blood.

In terms of the divisions of rakta, it has eight main ingredients, which can be further divided into thirty-five subsidiary ingredients. The thirty-five subsidiary ingredients are the five raktas composed of the four inner main ingredients and four outer main ingredients, the five wooden raktas, the five of stone, the five of flowers, the five root raktas, the five resultant raktas, and the five extracted raktas. Māhā-rakta, mūla-rakta, and guhya-rakta are extremely important. "Māhā-rakta" refers to blood from the liberation of the evil one. However, as a mere support for the visualization in the present context, it is permissible to use the clean blood of any living being, like a yak or a goat. "Mūla-rakta" refers to the root from which the world and its beings are formed. Still, clean water mixed with any of the red medicinal substances mentioned above will suffice. "Guhya-rakta" actually refers to rakta from an authentic lotus that has not been stained by sexual union. However, if that is unavailable, or seems unacceptable, in the context of blessing the *sindhūra* and rakta one visualizes rakta flowing from the secret place of Kīrti. This wisdom rakta flows into the ocean of samaya rakta where it dissolves and is absorbed.

As a side remark, the twelve links of dependent origination are a condensation or the root of the rakta, which is called "mūla-rakta." These twelve links of dependent origination, the causes and conditions for wandering through saṃsāra, can all be condensed into their root, ignorance. Consequently, ignorance can be completely uprooted by awareness wisdom. In this way, the recognition and full actualization of awareness wisdom will annihilate all seeds for cyclic existence. This is also known as the rakta that liberates from the six worlds of saṃsāra.

On all occasions, a practitioner of the unexcelled secret mantra should use the confidence of the view to resolve that saṃsāra and nirvāṇa are mind. Moreover, when experiencing the samādhi in which appearance and existence manifest as all-encompassing purity, the practitioner should use the strength of his disciplined conduct to bring all that occurs onto the path. This is the most important point.

The Secret Offerings

The secret offerings of unified bliss and emptiness consist of union and liberation.

In the offering of union, the subject is appearance—skillful means—and the object is emptiness—the wisdom consort. The indivisibility of these two through their primordial undivided union is the great primordial union. The taste of great bliss that emerges from this union satisfies all divine maṇḍalas. Visualize how the deities of the maṇḍala rest evenly in passionate desire, projecting blissful light rays that make offerings to the victorious ones. As the rays are reabsorbed, the secret empowerment is obtained. At this point, rest your mind in the wisdom of great bliss and generate the confidence of being indivisible from the passionate desire of the deities.

During the liberation offering one seeks to liberate all the dualistic thoughts that characterize the belief in a self. These are what propel us in cyclic existence and prevent the realization of nondual wisdom. The way to liberate them is to let the sharp sword of nonconceptual wisdom liberate the primordial belief in a personal self along with its concepts of attachment into unborn basic space. This is the great primordial liberation of everything. From within that state, imagine all the negative karmic acts accumulated by the ten types of errant sentient beings and consider how their acts will result in unbearable suffering. Now, in order to protect those beings, first motivate yourself with great compassion. Then you must realize that, essentially, neither you nor those whom you will liberate possess even a tiny bit of reality. Instead, you are like an illusion or a hallucination. Then, think that you perform the liberation and offer their concepts into the pure expanse of the equal taste of saṃsāra and nirvāṇa within the basic space of phenomena. You liberate yourself through realization and others through compassion. Therefore, from your own heart center the syllable RAṂ is emanated. Blazing with wisdom, it burns up the six seed syllables in the hearts of the ones you are liberating, together with their habitual tendencies. In this way, their consciousness is liberated into the basic space of phenomena.

The Offering of Suchness

All phenomena of saṃsāra and nirvāṇa, everything that appears and exists, is primordially and naturally pure as the spontaneously present maṇḍala of the victorious ones. Therefore, you should bring to mind the meaning of the Great Perfection, the natural state, which is devoid of even the slightest reality and free from focus on the giver, the recipient, and the act of offering. This is the offering of the Great Seal, the absence of concepts of subject, object, and action. From among all offerings, this is unparalleled.

Praises

Following the offerings, you should recall the great qualities of the maṇḍala deities. Then, with deep faith, praise them while making the appropriate gestures. *The Karma-māle* says:

Wield the vajra and ring the bell.
Ring the bell with the gestures of the five families.

Accordingly, make the gestures while holding the bell. In this context, OṂ represents the supreme knowledge among all bodhisattvas, and therefore the text says "supreme!" In fact, the form of the vajra master is none other than a manifestation of the five wisdoms, which are: (1) the wisdom of the basic space of phenomena, which is also the wisdom of knowing things as they are, (2) the mirrorlike wisdom, which refers to the wisdom of knowing all that exists, (3) the wisdom of equality, (4) discerning wisdom, and (5) all-accomplishing wisdom. In this way, the vajra master embodies the highest knowledge and the most excellent glory within existence and peace—the unity of space and awareness. Moreover, in essence he spontaneously accomplishes the seven riches of the view.

In general, all knowledge holders can be classified in terms of the four knowledge holders. According to this system, the great knowledge holder Pema Tötreng Tsal is primarily considered a spontaneously accomplished knowledge holder. According to the account of his liberation, he demonstrated the attainment of a common knowledge holder in the Kakyong cave. Then, at the Maratika cave, he attained the inconceivable power over death and conquered the four fears that are present on the seven impure grounds. In this way, he demonstrated the accomplishment of a knowledge holder with power over longevity dwelling on the eighth ground. Later, at Yangleshö he actualized the levels of a knowledge holder of the great seal and a spontaneously accomplished knowledge holder. In this way, he attained the supreme accomplishment and became the great ultimate paṇḍita. Subsequently, in Bodhgaya, he became empowered as the regent of the Victorious One and greatly proclaimed the sound of the dharma with inexhaustible courage. Thus he was victorious over the four demons and all non-Buddhists. It is him that we praise.

Likewise, with respect to the master Mañjuśrī, he is the source of the mind generation of all of the victorious ones of the three times and is thus called "Mañjuśrī, only father." The goddess Sarasvatī, "the mother who gives birth to all victorious ones," is the mother from whom all victorious ones are born. This is because the melodious speech of the expressive eighty-four thousand dharma teachings originates from the expressed, the mother of emptiness. Therefore, when they manifest as the four families to guide all those in need, they take the form of male and female deities in order to indicate the unity of the wisdom of emptiness and the method of great bliss. The magical emanation is the male and the net appears as the female deity. Although they are of one essence, they appear in various displays, such as the four families as well as the inconceivable maṇḍalas of the lesser families and the activity emanations that take a worldly form, such as the four kings and their attendants. Praise all the deities in the entire maṇḍala.

Focusing on the Appearance of the Deity

This section has five topics: (1) clear appearance, (2) stable confidence, (3) recollection of purity, (4) appearing as bliss, clarity, and emptiness, and (5) the measure of progress in training.

Clear appearance is obtained by visualizing the entire body of the deity all at once and then concentrating on that. Alternatively, one can visualize the various body parts and ornaments one at a time, from the top ornament down to the throne. When you have visualized each of the parts clearly and are able to generate the entire visualization all at once, you should rest your mind one-pointedly in equanimity on its limpid clarity, which is like a reflection in a stainless pool, unruffled by the wind.

Stable confidence is to recognize that you are the very deity that you meditate on—a buddha, who has purified all faults and developed all good qualities. If that vivid confidence is embraced by a mind free from grasping, the practice becomes an authentic unity of the development and completion stages. The recollection of purity has already been explained above at the occasion of developing the deity, and here, as one meditates, it should be applied in the same manner. Training in bliss, clarity, and emptiness requires that the pure, clear, and stable development stage is free from any concepts of grasping it as being real. Instead, one must embrace the visualization with the knowledge that its essence is empty and its nature is apparent yet not truly existing, just like a rainbow or the reflection of the moon in water. Sealing the development stage with the completion stage is an amazing skillful method by which all maṇḍalas arise as the dharma body.

Finally, regarding the measure of progress in training, the chapter on the root samādhi of the quintessence of unimpeded wisdom, found in *The Essence Manual of Oral Instructions* teaches:

> Having practiced one-pointedly in that way,
> The meditative experiences of movement, attainment,
> familiarity, stability, and completion will arise,
> And the divine form, with threefold clarity, is truly met.

As explained here, sometimes the visualization will be very clear and other times not at all. That is the experience of *movement*. When your visualization is always clear, that is the experience of *attainment*. Although during this experience your visualization is clear whenever you meditate, there comes a time when the clarity remains undiminished for as long as you meditate, and not just for a short time. That is the experience of *familiarity*. Later, when you are never separated from the clear appearance of the deity whether during equipoise or the ensuing attainment, that is the experience of *stability*.

When you are never apart from appearing as the deity, whether during equipoise or the ensuing attainment, the vivid mental appearance is a *mental object*. Later, when the deity can be clearly experienced with your senses, so that it can be touched and seen, it is an *apparent object*. Finally, when all impure appearances, indicated by your own body, disappear and the clear appearance of the deity and the confidence of being the deity arise one-pointedly as an *actual object*, this is the final experience of *completion*. The fruition of the development stage system is that all impure appearances are purified into the pure maṇḍala of the support and the supported.

Enlightened Speech: The Practice of Recitation

There are three types of mantra: (1) the root mantra, the unmistaken cause, (2) the conditional mantra for development, and (3) the activity mantra for recitation. Here, we are dealing with the final category.

Apart from the occasions of accomplishment and great accomplishment, such as during approach and the daily practice, it is not required to divide the recitation mansion. However, whether short or long, the session should always have three parts: (1) approaching the enlightened body by bringing forth the clear appearance of the deity's form, (2) approaching the enlightened speech by projecting and absorbing while focusing on the intent of recitation, and (3) approaching the enlightened mind by resting in the equanimity of suchness. This is mentioned in *The Essence Manual of Oral Instructions*:

> In every session, focus on the clear appearance of the deity.
> In every session, plant the great stake of the essence mantra.
> In every session, rest in the equality of your mind and the deity.
> In every session, produce miracles by projecting and absorbing light.

During approach, the recitation is like a moon with a garland of stars. For close approach, the recitation is like a spinning firebrand or a palanquin. During accomplishment, it is like the king's messenger, a dispatched servant. Finally, for great accomplishment, the recitation is like a broken beehive. During each of these four occasions, you should know which recitation is the appropriate one.

The deities should be aroused for the recitation with the verse:

> HŪṂ HRĪḤ Deities who play as illusory wisdom.

In the heart center of Guru Vādisiṃha, the lord of the maṇḍala, is a full moon disc that supports a white syllable HRĪḤ. This syllable stands upright, facing outward. You can visualize it either being flat or three-dimensional. It is surrounded by the main mantra OṂ ĀḤ HŪṂ VAJRA GURU PADMA PRAJÑĀ JÑĀNA SARVA SIDDHI HŪṂ. The mantra syllables face outward and are arranged counterclockwise.

In the heart center of each of the four forms of Mañjuśrī is a moon disc that supports the syllable DHĪḤ. The syllable has the same color as its respective deity. It is encircled by his mantra with the letters facing outward, in a counterclockwise arrangement. In the heart center of each of the four forms of Sarasvatī is a sun disc that supports a syllable HRĪḤ. The syllable has the same color as its respective deity. It is surrounded by her mantra, which faces inward and is arranged clockwise. In the heart center of each of the four great kings is a sun disc. This disc supports the first syllable of the life-force mantra or, alternatively, the syllable BAI. The respective mantras surround the seed syllables, facing outward in a counterclockwise manner.

Above, the intent of recitation that is like a moon with a garland of stars was mentioned. Here the life-force syllable is like the moon, and the surrounding mantra is like the twinkling stars. Direct your awareness one-pointedly to this without wavering from it and perform all three types of silent and actual recitation.

During close approach, the recitation is like a spinning firebrand. Here you should first divide the recitation mansion. Then you should visualize the mantras for the main deity, together with the four families of Mañjuśrī and the attendant four great kings. These are all arranged counterclockwise, while the mantras for the four families of Sarasvatī are arranged clockwise. Then, the mantra garland at Vādisiṃha's heart center emanates a second mantra garland. The syllables in these garlands are lined up without directly touching each other but also not leaving any space in between them. The mantra garland, together with its sounds, emerges from the mouth of the samaya being and enters the mouth of the wisdom being in front of you. Passing through the body, it emerges from the navel point of the deity generated in front and from there enters again into the navel point of the self-created form of the deity. As the mantra chain dissolves into the seed syllable in the deity's heart center, imagine that supreme wisdom-knowledge is unfolded.

The intent of recitation that is like the king's servant involves two types of visualization. These are the visualization of gathering blessings for the benefit of oneself and the all-pervading enlightened activity for the benefit of others. For the four families of Mañjuśrī, one should begin with the visualization of enlightened activity for the benefit of others the way it is clarified in the treasure text. Imagine that the mantra garland in the heart center spins and projects light rays that touch all sentient beings of the six classes. The light purifies their stains of ignorance, the root of all karma and negative emotions, and brings them enlightenment by transforming their body, speech, and mind into the essence of the three vajras.

Once again, five-colored light radiates out, filling space with pleasing offerings to all the victorious ones and their offspring. The light unfolds the wisdom and qualities of the noble bodhisattvas, listeners, and self-realized buddhas as well as of ordinary beings so that it equals space. Imagine that all their blessings and spiritual accomplishments and, in particular, all the strength of their intelligence takes on the form of light rays and dissolves into your heart center. In this way, the light of wisdom that knows all things, as well as their nature, shines like the sun and purifies all ignorance.

The light rays that the forms of Mañjuśrī and Sarasvatī project and absorb have the same color as their respective deity. Here one should be mindful of visualizing an increase in their respective wisdoms related to teaching, debating, and composition.

During the recitation for the attendant four great kings, light rays are projected from the heart center of the central deity, touching the heart center of each of the four attendants and inspiring them. The light then causes their intelligence and courageous eloquence, along with that of those under their dominion, to dissolve into oneself. Additionally, imagine that the essence of all the strength, splendor, riches, and elixirs of the gods, sages, sorcerers, nāgās, spirits, as well as the sun, the moon, and the planets is gathered and dissolves into you. As the strength of their intelligence and splendor has dissolved into you, you attain the confidence to outshine Brahma, the lord of the form realm.

During the practice of great accomplishment, the visualization is like a broken beehive. Here bodies like the main deity's are projected, filling space like a mass of mustard seeds or like particles of dust in the sunlight. As they perform their vajra dances, the tune of the recitation of enlightened speech resounds like a broken hive of bees. From within the luminous state of the unchanging enlightened mind, offering clouds of good qualities fill the buddha fields of the ten directions and make offerings to all victorious ones and their offspring. As the continuity of offerings is unbroken, it is also an offering to the buddhas of the three times. *The Vajra Sequence* teaches:

> To the buddhas of the ten directions and their offspring,
> As well as the lords, the buddhas of the present,
> And sentient beings who have the nature of future buddhas,
> I offer this body for the three purposes
> So that it may become a vessel for supreme qualities.

Thus, make offerings to the buddhas of the past, who now abide as buddhas in the pure realms of the ten directions, along with their offspring. Likewise, offer to the present buddhas, who are the lords and the masters. Finally, make offerings to the buddhas of the future, who are all sentient beings viewed as yidam deities.

Enlightened activity, such as guiding beings and performing the twelve deeds, is limitless and therefore it can fully purify the two obscurations in the three realms. Manifesting as empowerment deities of the three complete seats, the deities of the maṇḍala use the vase to confer the empowerment of nectar by means of bodhicitta. Everyone is awakened into the form of the deities of the three roots, and the outer world becomes the pure realm of the unexcelled vajra space. All appearances are the great forms of the deities' enlightened bodies. All sounds and voices are the wisdom play of the deities' mantras. All thoughts are the samādhi of nondual wisdom. All of appearance and existence is primordially manifest from the ground as the essence of deity, mantra, and wisdom.

From within the clarity of this experience, perform the visualization as it is described in the recitation section of the *Condensed Activity* manual:

> I and the deities of the maṇḍala manifest bodies from our bodies to fill all the world.

Then perform the recitation for the main deity and the retinue. In the context of the daily practice, approach and accomplishment are practiced together as a sort of devoted training. Therefore, with regard to elements such as the spinning of the mantra chain and the projection and absorption of light, one should just follow the visualization for the recitation as it is outlined in the practice manual. The explanation of when to divide the recitation mansion is clearly described in the instruction manual for *The Secret Essence of Vajrasattva*, so you may study it there.

A profound key point of recitation is to place the mind one-pointedly in samādhi, without being distracted by thoughts. Padmasambhava described this:

> Recite with undistracted concentration.
> Should you become distracted elsewhere,
> Even reciting for an eon will bring no result.

The rosary that is used to count the recitations should also have certain characteristics. They are mentioned in the section on clarifying the rosary from *The Condensed Realization of the Gurus*:

> For a rosary, the best substances are jewels.
> Seeds that come from trees are second best.
> The lowest are wood, stones,
> And the nine types of medicine.
>
> Conch makes for peaceful rosaries
> And is recommended for pacifying activities.

Golden rosaries are used for enriching activities,
While rosaries of coral accomplish magnetizing activities.

Rosaries of iron and turquoise are for wrathful activities.
Zi and agate are auspicious for various activities.
Bodhi seeds are auspicious for all activities.
Ivory rosaries accomplish all activities.

With respect to the different degrees of benefit, *The Vajra Peak Tantra* says:

Lotus is said to multiply by one billion,
And the bodhi seed to do so infinitely.

Thus, for peaceful deities it is good to use bodhi seeds, while for wrathful deities rudrākṣa is recommended. In particular, Drubwang Chagme Rinpoche mentions in his *Precious Six-Faced Mañjuśrī* that golden rosaries, which are so renowned these days, are excellent for practicing Mañjuśrī. However, one should use whatever is comfortable. *The Tantra of the Natural Arising of Awareness* describes the string of the rosary and the main bead:

For the rosary, join three, five, or nine strings
Symbolizing the three bodies, five families, and nine vehicles.
The knots are bound by three tiers of beads, symbolizing the three bodies.

Thus it is acceptable to use three, five, or nine strings bound together. Additionally, it is good to use white woolen thread for peaceful activity, yellow cotton thread for enriching activity, red silk thread for magnetizing activities, while for wrathful activity knife-leather or great leather are recommended. However, if you cannot gather these, regular leather will do. For multiple activities, use five threads of different colors. *The Condensed Realization* mentions this:

The rosary string for various activities
Is a braided string of five colored threads.

Generally, the rosary should have three tiers of knots to symbolize the three bodies. The upper one is blue to symbolize vajra mind, the unchanging basic space of phenomena. The middle one is red to symbolize vajra speech, while the lower one is white to symbolize vajra body.

The rosary should be blessed by following the elevenfold preliminary blessing. The method for counting mantras is explained in *The Condensed Realization of the Gurus*:

When reciting peaceful mantras,
Count with the rosary on your index finger,
And for enriching mantras on your middle finger.
For magnetizing, keep it on your ring finger,
And for wrathful mantras, on the little finger.
Always use your left hand.

Although this is what the text explains, sometimes it is also said that for wrathful mantras one should use the thumb and ring finger of the right hand. However, for general practice of all four activities, you can recite with the four fingers held together, the rosary resting on the index finger and the thumb acting like an iron hook.

Padmasambhava also taught where to hold one's hand during the recitation:

Count at your heart for peaceful activity,
At your navel for enriching activity,
At the secret place for magnetizing activity,
And for wrathful activity, near your knee
At the point where the legs are crossed.
For various activities, count wherever is easy.

The Condensed Realization teaches many samaya vows relating to the rosary. The most important point, however, is to prevent the rosary from being held by an obscured person with damaged samaya vows or someone who has caused a rift against the samaya vows.

When you recite, do not recite each syllable overly quickly or slowly, or mix up the length of the syllables. Do not break the recitation with any other words, even with the recitation of another mantra. Additionally, some learned masters have mentioned in their recitation manuals that if you slip into conversation while reciting, you must go back four beads on the rosary. If you cough, go back five, three if you yawn, ten if you sneeze, and one if you spit. Since this is what has been taught, we should not disregard it but take it into consideration.

Generally, in terms of the number of recitations, one should recite one hundred thousand mantras for each syllable of the mantra of the main deity of the maṇḍala and one-tenth of that for each of the deities in the retinue. In all cases, one must add a 10 percent amendment, which means reciting an extra ten thousand mantras for every hundred thousand repetitions and one thousand extra for every ten thousand. For Guru Vādisiṃha, the treasure revealer himself previously said that ideally one should recite one hundred million mantras, although ten million recitations are also good. The minimum is seven or four hundred thousand mantras, while one hundred thousand is just enough to make a connection.

The duration of the practice is mentioned in *The Essence Manual of Oral Instructions*, which says:

> The time for completion is six, twelve, or eighteen months.

Accordingly, the practice takes six months for persons of superior faculties to complete, twelve months for those of middling faculties, and eighteen months for those of lesser faculties. However, with respect to this particular form of Mañjuśrī, the following is also mentioned:

> It only takes between one month and half a year before one directly beholds the faces of the guru and his retinue of

> Mañjuśrī and Sarasvatī, hears the sound of their mantras, and gives birth to samādhi and wisdom. In dreams one will receive signs, such as discovering representations of enlightened body, speech, and mind, watching the rise of the sun and moon, encountering flowers and fruits, large rivers expanding, and fires blazing. Thus, one's intelligence will improve.

You will experience all this directly, just as described. Additionally, *The Essence Manual of Oral Instructions* mentions the following signs of accomplishment:

> The outer signs are directly seeing the deity's face,
> Light shining from the maṇḍala, the nectar vase boiling,
> The skull cup blazing, and candles burning on their own.
> The inner signs are bliss in body, speech, and mind, and clear energies and awareness,
> As well as seeing subject and object as illusory.
> As the secret sign, in one-pointed meditative concentration,
> Realization is unchanging and perfected within the state of the deity.
> At that moment, the supreme spiritual accomplishment is manifest,
> Appearance and mind become one, and various miracles are displayed.
> Although your body remains the same, your mind is accomplished
> As the form of the deity—the matured knowledge holder.
> Transforming into the vajra body, you attain power of longevity.
> Stable within the supreme class of the five types of the great seal,
> You perfect the tenth level and become a great regent
> Manifesting as the spontaneously present knowledge holder.

While you may choose to recite the mantra for a fixed number of repetitions, it is better to recite for a certain duration of time. Ideally, however, one should recite until the proper signs appear. Vimalamitra mentions this in *The Radiant Garland*:

> The supreme skillful method is said to be recitation in terms of number, time, and signs.

It is therefore important to continue until you have perfected the practice. Moreover, the masters mention that one can use the hundred-syllable mantra to make up for any faults in your recitation. They also mention that one should recite in a clear tune to generate strength. Later, one should stabilize that strength through the mantra of the essence of dependent origination. Lastly, while visualizing all the deities of the maṇḍala, one should make offerings, utter praises, and make confessions after every thousand repetitions. Then, chant the verse:

> HŪṂ Host of wisdom deities . . .

Supplicating

The reason for supplicating is to achieve one's aims. In this context, you should first utter the syllable OṂ, which represents a request for the supreme gift. Then you should supplicate Guru Vādisiṃha, who is the embodiment of the supreme knowledge of all the buddhas and their offspring, the pervasive lord of all families, and the sublime identity of great bliss and luminosity. Following that, supplicate the entire gathering of deities who manifest as the maṇḍala of the magical net in the form of means and knowledge, indivisible from Guru Vādisiṃha. Request them to pay heed to you, the practitioner. Having made this petition, exhort them to grant the blessings of great compassion. Your request for spiritual accomplishments should be as follows:

> In a spontaneous and effortless manner, may the light of the highest knowledge and wisdom fully dawn within me. In the same way, may I be granted total recall, unwavering mindfulness, clairvoyance to know what is otherwise hid-

> den, and the ability to rest one-pointedly in samādhi. From this day on until I reach the essence of enlightenment, may Guru Vādisiṃha himself be my spiritual guide and, with his immensely loving enlightened mind, liberate me from the two extremes of existence and peace. May I attain the sacred state where the light of omniscient wisdom perceives all phenomena as a nonconceptual and natural clarity, just like reflections in a mirror, without any conceptual ideas related to their existence or lack thereof.

In this way, you should pray with a one-pointed mind.

Part Three: The Conclusion

For the concluding activities, first comes an explanation of the gathering offering.

The Gathering Offering

When organizing the gathering, there are many profound instructions related to the authentic gathering circle. However, if that is what you want to practice, you should learn it elsewhere. Therefore, here I will give only a brief explanation of the stages of visualization for the basic gathering offering as it is commonly practiced these days.

For this, arrange as much food and drink for the gathering as you can afford. Then begin by sprinkling them with nectar. Visualize yourself as the deity and imagine that the syllables RAṂ, YAṂ, and KHAṂ radiate forth from your heart center and respectively burn, scatter, and wash away all impurities in the offering substances. Then, in a vast and expansive skull vessel, the five meats and five nectars dissolve into light. On top of this light are the syllables OṂ, ĀḤ, and HŪṂ. These syllables project light that gathers wisdom nectar and dissolves it into the offerings. As that occurs, goddesses with pleasing offerings emanate from clouds in the middle of that great ocean, filling space.

As you extend an invitation with three HŪṂ syllables, the deities of the three roots manifest from the basic space of luminosity, led by the gatherings of deities in the maṇḍalas of the oceanlike victorious ones of the three bodies, filling all of space. Think that, although the deities never stray from the basic space of the essence of the dharma body, their form bodies appear as a play of illusory wisdom in order to purify the two obscurations and complete the two accumulations for all sentient beings, including you. The words VAJRA SAMĀJAḤ invoke the unchanging aspirations that the deities have made in the past, so that they arrive in order to benefit those who need guidance.

For the first offering, say OṂ ĀḤ HŪṂ and then imagine that the essence of these syllables—the wisdom of enlightened body, speech, and mind—takes the form of nectar. This nectar is then offered by goddesses of the five sense pleasures, who fill all of space. With this enjoyment of undefiled great bliss, the host of deities of the three roots are pleased. When you say, SARVA GAṆACAKRA PŪJĀ HOḤ, it means "May the complete gathering circle be pleased." The meaning of the complete gathering circle can be condensed into four parts. These are the outer gathering circle of the sense pleasures, the inner blissful melting of the aggregates and elements, the secret union of means and knowledge, and the suchness gathering circle of nondual coemergent wisdom.

The next stage is confession. Here, HOḤ is a request to the deities to be heard. Having uttered that, you should confess and make amendments for all evil deeds, obscurations, and transgressions that you have accumulated in general since time without beginning. In particular, however, you should confess and make amendments for all transgressions, damages, breaches, and infractions of both the main and the subsidiary samaya vows. Do this by offering the gathering of sense pleasures to the host of deities of the maṇḍala. SAMAYA ŚUDDHE ĀḤ means "may the samaya vows become pure." Then think that all of your downfalls and stains have been purified and rejoice.

Third is the liberation. As you utter HŪṂ, the whole world becomes a blazing wheel with ten spokes, and all sentient beings living there are visualized as the host of deities of Wrathful Mañjuśrī, while you become the Great Glorious One. From your heart center, numerous arresting emissaries are emanated throughout space. In their hands they hold hooks, lassos, shackles, and bells. Capturing all of types of dualistic rudras, demons, and obstructing forces, they bring them in front of you. Through the samādhi of the three liberations, they are ushered into the triangle, the syllable E.

Next, numerous liberating emissaries are emanated from your heart center, brandishing various weapons, such as kīlas, vajras, swords, and hammers. These weapons are created by the play of nondual wisdom and, as they strike and cleave, the aggregates are liberated. As the consciousness in the form of a black TRI syllable is struck by the weapons, it turns into a white A syllable, which dissolves into your heart center. At that point, rest in the equanimity of the wisdom of luminosity, free from concepts of someone liberated and one who liberates.

Before the weapons are planted, the ritual substances should be visualized as weapons and sprinkled with rakta. Following the liberation, sprinkle them with nectar. Thus, though the essence of the offering is the nectar of wisdom, it takes the form of flesh, blood, and bones, which are offered to the gathering of deities by the offering emissaries who hold triangular ladles. As the maṇḍala deities consume the offering with great relish, visualize that the three poisons are liberated into the expanse of enlightened body, speech, and mind.

The mantra SARVA VIGHNĀN ŚATRŪN MĀRAYA KHA KHA KHĀHI KHĀHI means, "Kill all enemies and obstructing forces. Please enjoy this! You must enjoy this!" The deities are pleased with the liberation offering and joyfully exclaim "ha ha hi hi." As you utter HŪṂ, the emissaries dissolve into you. Then repeat the HŪṂ and rest in luminosity. Finally, by saying PHAṬ, the one who was liberated is brought into basic space.

Next, one should enjoy the gathering. For this, the vajra assistant holds the food in his right hand and the drink in his left. He then offers it, saying, "Enjoy the gathering offering as an adornment!" This signifies that one does not abandon the sense pleasures but enjoys them as an adornment of wisdom. Everyone should receive the feast with the lotus gesture and say "a-la-la ho!" This shows one's amazement at such wonderful methods.

It is said that the supreme spiritual accomplishment is obtained by drinking *madāna* and that the spiritual accomplishment of immortality comes by enjoying life, while strength and power is brought about by enjoying maṃsa. Knowing the aggregates, elements, and sense sources to be deities of the three complete seats, enjoy the nectar of wisdom and imagine that it pleases the deities who abide in the center of your body.

While partaking of the gathering, you should not think of the food in terms of clean or dirty, good or bad. Do not engage in blame, reproach, disparagement, argument, or even amusement. If you commit faults, such as eating excessively and hoarding, it is said that you will be reborn as a pernicious being living in a graveyard, such as a corpse-eating jackal—so be careful.

Next, gather the residuals. When doing so, it is auspicious to place all of the clean residuals on top of the dirty residuals. On the other hand, it is very powerful yet inauspicious to place all the dirty residuals on top of the clean ones. Thus, to avoid the flaw of the latter approach while keeping its positive aspect, first place a piece of the dirty residuals on top of the clean residuals. Then, blend the clean residuals with the dirty residuals before placing a piece of the deity torma on top. Take this before the master. The teachings say that he should sprinkle it with a bit of his saliva, so you actually need a qualified vajra master for this. However, at this degenerate time when it seems that ritual activities are often practiced incorrectly, even the precious great treasure revealer declined to do this. Therefore, there is no need to even consider anyone else practicing like that.

The vajra master makes the gesture of the source of phenomena, also called the samaya seal, over the residual offering. The vajra assistant then places it on a tripod at the end of the row, just like in the context of the extensive practice manual. In most practices of the Transmitted Teachings, it is clarified that it should be placed to the southeast of the maṇḍala. First sprinkle nectar followed by rakta and then make a petition. Next, set up a glorious flame there, but don't move the residual offering around before it is time to offer it. While playing music, lift the residuals with the garuda gesture, carry them a vajra stride away, and pour them out in a heap onto a clean place on the ground.

If you scatter the residuals, it will bring about faults such as widespread sickness and calamity. So instead pour them out in a heap and, keeping the mouth of the residual offering vessel facing toward the practitioners, take the vessel back inside. If you carry it back inside with the vessel's mouth pointed outward, the accomplishments will be scattered, so avoid doing that. If the tray for the gathering is washed, the accomplishments will diminish, so you may place it anywhere you like but avoid washing it. In the context of the *Extensive Activity*, the rinsing water for the enjoining torma and the throwing torma should be poured on the torma for the Tenma goddesses before it is offered. At the end of the ritual for the enjoining torma, the throwing torma, and the reversal of negative energies, the vessel should be placed upside down. Then, the master presses down a vajra on top of this vessel and crosses it. It is also best to turn the vessel for the Tenma goddesses upside down. At the completion of the Hayagrīva dance, immediately turn the torma vessel upright and scatter flowers. Then make supplications for the long life of the masters and chant various aspirations.

At this point you should visualize that the gathering torma transforms into a great swirling ocean of wisdom nectar. Then, the nectar of awakened mind of Hayagrīva and consort, who rest in union on the tip of your tongue, emanates the syllables OṂ ĀḤ HŪṂ. These syllables dissolve into the ocean of nectar, purifying all impurities and blessing it as the nectar of wisdom.

As the guests to whom the residual offering is made are subjugated, call out BHYŌ. Then recite the verse:

Servants of the Great Glorious One, host of messengers . . .

At this point the oath-bound worldly protectors, who abide by the commands and their commitments, come to consume the residuals. These protectors include the twenty-eight iśvaras, the thirty-two ḍākinīs, the eighteen great emissaries, the sixteen rākśasas, the eight fiery beings, the seven mothers, the four sisters, the three-hundred and sixty servants, the four great kings, the protectors of the ten directions, the eight nāgās and eight deities, the deities of the eight planets and twenty-eight stars together with the nine frightful ones, the seventy-five glorious protectors, the twelve Tenma goddesses, and the thirteen mountain gods. Having consumed the residuals, they are pleased and satisfied. Earlier, in the presence of the Glorious One, they said:

> We will not enjoy the first serving but the leftovers.
> We do not seek the center but will protect the boundaries
> Of this great gathering maṇḍala.

The Glorious One then placed them as principal among those who are mere members of the gathering. Thus, in accordance with their commitments, they eradicate all of the obstructing conditions for the practitioner and increase conducive circumstances, just as they have been entreated to do. Think that this is what has happened.

As for the meaning of the mantra, MA MA is the primary life-force mantra of the mamo goddesses, HRĪṂ HRĪṂ is an incantation, and BALIṂTA KHĀHI means, "Eat the torma." Thus, the mantra is a request for the mamo goddesses to arrive and eat the torma. The guests of the residual offering then return to their own places. Then, visualize the peaceful maṇḍala and make offerings and praises to the field of accumulation in front of you while also requesting forgiveness.

At the end of the practice, such as on the final day, you should take the accomplishments. At that time, visualize that white, red, and blue light rays stream forth from the three places of the deities in the field of accumulation and dissolve into the substances that confer spiritual accomplishment, such as the five nectars, so that they turn into the nectar of enlightened body, speech, and mind. Then, visualize the field of accomplishment dissolving into you as you recite the following verses:

> HŪṂ HRĪḤ In the essence maṇḍala of bodhicitta . . .
> The constitution of the channels is cleaned and filled with
> nectar.

The Concluding Activities

The Dissolution of the Development Stage

The main text of the extensive practice manual says:

> The expression of unborn emptiness arises
> As the maṇḍala deities of the great magical display.
> As they all dissolve in you,
> Rest in the perfect state beyond focus.

Then, utter HŪṂ HŪṂ HŪṂ and visualize how the world and its contents dissolve into the protection circle and so on until finally the tip of the seed syllable itself dissolves. (First, the outer pure world and its contents dissolve into light and dissolve into the protection circle. Then, the gradually stacked elements, the protection circle, the charnel grounds and the other outer parts dissolve into the celestial palace. In turn, the palace dissolves into the retinue, which dissolves into the principal deity. The principal deity dissolves into the moon disc at his heart. Finally, the moon disc dissolves into the syllable HRĪḤ, which dissolves from the bottom up until even the upper tip is gone.)

Alternatively, the wisdom maṇḍala of supreme knowledge—the world and its contents—dissolves into clarity. The principal deity dissolves into the letter HRĪḤ at his heart center. Finally, even that is not observed and one rests in luminosity.

Emptiness is not something that can be established as either self or other. It cannot be observed in any way, and so no existence, nonexistence, being or nonbeing is seen. As such, emptiness is completely free from all conceptual activity. As you rest in equanimity in this state, it clears away the extreme of permanence. Then, to clear away the extreme of nihilism, say PHAṬ PHAṬ PHAṬ, which acts as a circumstance for Guru Vādisiṃha to reappear, like a fish jumping out of the water.

Moreover, concerning the main points for particular visualizations, when you set out to compose an important treatise, visualize that your body as the principal deity transforms during the ensuing attainment and takes on the form of White Mañjuśrī. When memorizing dharma texts, it should be Vāgīśvara and, when teaching, Vādirāṭ. For writing, Vajratīkṣṇa is suitable if you wish your knowledge to increase. Vajra Sarasvatī is for sharpness and clarity, Ratna Sarasvatī for stable intelligence, Padma Sarasvatī for intelligence to become deep like an ocean, and Karma Sarasvatī for intelligence to be vast like the sky.

When reciting the mantras for these individual deities, it is good to know the individual attainments that they produce. This meaning is mentioned in the treasure text where it says "Clear as the seals of enlightened body, speech, and mind." Additionally, the *Subsequent Activity* text mentions:

> With the armor of the indestructible vajra,
> The maṇḍala deities in the palace of appearance and existence,
> Within the state of the great magical net,
> Continuously act for the benefit of beings.
> The bodies and wisdoms are spontaneously present.

Here "vajra armor" refers to resting in the samādhi where one's body, speech, and mind are the three vajras. This is expressed in the statement VAJRA KA VĀ CI RAKṢA 'HAṂ. (Protect my vajra body, speech, and mind.) As you say OṂ ĀḤ HŪṂ, make the five-pointed vajra gesture and touch your three places. At that point, visualize that your crown is marked with an OṂ, your throat with an ĀḤ, and your heart center with the syllable HŪṂ.

Moreover, within the state in which the entire world is the celestial palace of great liberation and all beings are the great magical net of Mañjuśrī, investigate the pure nature of mind, the innate state. No matter how much you examine, you will not find that it is an actual thing or something truly existent, nor can it be identified as appearance or awareness. At that point, simply rest within this naked state, which has no object apart from self-cognizance—this self-arisen wisdom, the indivisibility of the two truths, beyond conceptual mind. Don't push yourself by being too rigid, don't be overly loose, and avoid any attempts to make the state clear or focused. Instead, simply remain in the natural state, just as it is. If you rest your awareness vividly in nondual self-cognizance without moving from that state, that itself is the unity of calm abiding and insight. If you never part from this very view and meditation, all your experiences and activities will facilitate the coemergent wisdom of great bliss. That is the conduct.

Know that appearances, sounds, and thoughts are deities, mantra, and wisdom. Walking, sitting, moving, and all activities are the deity's mudrās. Eating and drinking should be performed as the practice of sustenance, such as with the actions of internal burning and pouring. The entire array of desired objects should be taken as supports for the path by not forming concepts of subject, object, and action. Thus, whether you are sleeping or awake, make sure that your practice activity is always meaningful.

Aspiration Prayers

With respect to aspiration prayers, the precious guru of Uḍḍiyāṇa said:

> Motivated by faith and compassion,
> And for the sake of others' welfare—the mind of awakening,
> I dedicate and make aspirations.

In the same way, with the attitude of the mind of awakening, make pure aspirations that you will be able to benefit others on a vast scale. HO is an exclamation that indicates wonder. As you utter that, consider how wonderful it is that you have been able to gather such great amounts of basic goodness. Rejoice in this achievement and raise your spirits as you recite the following verse:

> By the power of accomplishing the maṇḍala of the knowledge holder master . . .

Here, with respect to the four levels of the knowledge holder, the fruition, Master Buddhaguhya explained in *Stages of the Path*:

> As the defiled aggregates, elements, and sense sources are exhausted
> In the vajra body, one attains the knowledge holder with power over longevity.

As this applies to the Precious One himself, at Maratika Padmasambhava fully manifested the level of a knowledge holder with mastery over longevity and at Yangleshö he arrived at the level of a spontaneously present knowledge holder. *Stages of the Path* says:

> Thus, pure wisdom itself
> Is the vajra holder with the five bodies spontaneously present.

Accordingly, form the aspiration that the virtue resulting from practicing the maṇḍala of Vādisiṃha—the lord vajra holder who has spontaneously accomplished the five bodies—may be of benefit to all countless sentient beings, including yourself. In particular, form the wish that all beings may spontaneously accomplish the four types of enlightened activity—pacifying, enriching, magnetizing, and wrathful—and be liberated within the expanse of the dharma body of ultimate luminosity.

Verses of Auspiciousness

When reciting verses of auspiciousness, think that the victorious ones of the ten directions together with their offspring have arrived, filling all of space. They join in reciting the words of auspiciousness and a divine rain of flowers falls. The practitioners, visualizing themselves as deities during the breaks in between meditation sessions, also scatter flowers as they utter verses of auspiciousness.

Giving rise to a unique devotion regarding the meaning of the auspicious verses purifies samaya vows. This is because when giving rise to such devotion, the blessings of the root and lineage gurus definitely enter one. Accordingly, form the aspiration that the yidam deities and the ḍākinīs may accompany you like a shadow follows the body and that the dharma protectors and guardians may clear away obstacles. In this way, form the wish that there may be the auspiciousness of easily attaining the supreme and common spiritual accomplishments. While you utter such words of auspiciousness, scatter flowers. If you practice in this way, there is no doubt that your wishes will come to pass.

From the oceanlike profound treasure, *Accomplishing the Guru's Mind*,
Appears a method for accomplishing Mañjuśrī, shining in brilliant glory.
Forever manifesting the buddhas' teaching in the vast expanse of space,
It utterly dispels the darkness of delusion.

Thus blooms the lotus grove of the dharma of scripture,
And the sweet nectar of realization is enjoyed.
In that pleasure grove, a place of healing, shown by the profound treasure,
All bright and intelligent ones should gather.

The instructions of the vajra holder, the great treasure revealer,
I have here put in writing, as a reminder for my own practice,
Without corrupting them with any ideas of my own.
May the rivers of goodness flowing from this
Enter the ocean of the four omniscient bodies.

The topic of this text, *Blooming Intelligence*, is the means for practicing Guru Vādisiṃha. It is structured based on the *Condensed Activity* manual from *Accomplishing the Guru's Mind*. Arrogantly presuming this to be a full commentary on this practice, I structured the text in the same sequence that my guru, the great treasure revealer, explained.

Although the extensive practice manual is taught in twenty-one topics, for the sake of convenience I have here given a concise explanation that simply covers the preliminaries, the main part, and the conclusion. I wrote in this way, as I was worried that too many elaborations on the teaching for the actual treasure text might obscure the root text itself. Having received a command to compose these instructions, I respectfully offer these words. Moreover, having been most graciously requested to compose this text, I kept this encouragement foremost in my mind. Personally, I regard this yidam deity with particular devotion, and I believe that such an instruction is an indispensable condition for taking up this practice.

For these reasons, I began this composition at Yelphuk Namdzong Gyurme Ling, but some parts were not completed. Then, later, when the great knowledge holder master went to meet the two Jamgön Lamas at the Terchen Evam dharma encampment, I was requested by the lay tantric knowledge holders of Gato Par to continue writing. Accordingly, this was written with pure intention and respect by the treasure revealer's so-called disciple, Karma Sangye Chöpel, also known as Pema Drime Lodrö Shenphen Chökyi Nangwa. May there be the excellence of the teachings of the definitive secret essence spreading in one hundred directions!

Glorious Guru, I have a wish: may you remain firm for a hundred kalpas!

Blooming Intelligence

A Clarification of the Practice Manual of Guru Vādisiṃha
from the Cycle "Accomplishing the Guru's Mind:
Dispeller of All Obstacles"[1]

1. In preparing this translation, the translator gratefully consulted the earlier translation by Erik Pema Kunsang, *Blooming Intelligence: The Practice of Guru Mawey Senge, The Lion of Speech, according to the Tukdrup Barchey Künsel* (Kathmandu, Nepal: Rangjung Yeshe Publications, 1995).

Namo Guru Vādisiṃhāya!

I bow down before Guru Vādisiṃha,
The deity who vanquishes the dark ignorance of all beings
By spreading throughout all of space, the empty light of the two wisdoms
Free from the clouds of the two obscurations.

Those who wish to be freed from the darkness of existence
And to attain the brilliance of the authentic path
Rely upon this treasure, this essential amṛta,
A condensed method for accomplishing the profound and the vast!

This incredible and amazing secret that accomplishes the lord of superior knowledge, Guru Vādisiṃha, along with the yidam, Mañjuśrī and consort, in a single maṇḍala has three sections: 1) The practice manual, 2) the method for bestowing empowerment, and 3) the activity application. [Here only the practice manual is translated.]

For simply doing the main practice of the recitation that involves oneself visualized as the principal deity, elaborate preparation is not necessary. At dawn on an astrologically auspicious morning during the waxing moon, in a remote practice place, arrange whatever image of the deity you have. In front of this, simply place the white round torma, nectar, the two waters, and the seven offerings. Gather the preparatory torma and other requisite ritual items. Then, begin by reciting the seven-line supplication.

For the preparation, taking refuge, and generating the mind of awakening, recite these lines:

Namo!
I and all sentient beings equal to space
Take refuge in the supreme refuge objects
Generating the aspiring and applied mind of awakening
I will accomplish the level of Guru Vādisiṃha!

Say this three times. Consecrate the torma for the obstructers in the usual manner. Dedicate it with the mantra and say:

HŪṂ HRĪḤ
All demons, obstructers and evil spirits—dualistic deluded perceptions—
Take this torma and disperse to your own places.
Within this space of nondual wisdom, deity, mantra, and dharma body
The boundaries of the maṇḍala are naturally and spontaneously established.

HŪṂ HŪṂ HŪṂ

Say this and expel them by reciting wrathful mantras, playing music, and hurling ritual mustard seeds.

VAJRA RAKṢA RAKṢA BHRŪṂ

Say this and meditate on the protection circle. It is necessary to give the torma to the obstructers only the first time. Afterward, replace the words "Take this torma" from the verse above, with "Do not stay here, but." You also do not need to recite wrathful mantras. For the descent of blessings and consecration of the offering articles say:

OṂ ĀḤ HŪṂ
Vādisiṃha and your host of deities, manifest from space!

Bring blessings upon this place, bestow empowerment and accomplishments.
Bless this great offering mudrā of all that appears and exists, manifest within the ground,
To be an ocean of Samantabhadra's miraculously manifested offerings.
OṂ ĀḤ HŪṂ VAJRA GURU DEVA ḌĀKINĪ JÑĀNA ĀVEŚAYA ĀḤ ĀḤ

Saying this brings down the blessings.

HŪṂ HŪṂ HŪṂ

Saying this gathers the blessings.

OṂ SARVA PŪJĀ MEGHA ĀḤ HŪṂ

Say this three times, whereby the offering substances are greatly increased.

The beginning of the main part of practice is generating the deity:

ĀḤ
Within the dharma body, the luminous space of suchness,
Is the enjoyment body, compassion's unceasing, all-illuminating expression;
The emanation body, the seed samādhi, is the white letter HRĪḤ.
From this, light radiates forth, purifying clinging to a real world and beings.

Upon the gradually stacked elements in the center of the vajra protection circle,
BHRŪṂ becomes a jeweled celestial palace, completely perfect.
At its center, in the heart of a multicolored lotus, upon a sun and moon disc,
HRĪḤ transforms into Guru Vādisiṃha.

He is clear white, brilliant, and blazing with majesty.
His two hands at his heart center, in the gesture of teaching the dharma,
Hold the stems of two thousand-petaled lotuses that open by his ears.
On the right lotus rests a volume of text condensing the three baskets.

The left lotus is adorned with a volume of the Kīlaya tantra.
He is dressed as a fully ordained monk and wears a red paṇḍita hat.
He appears radiant, as the form of fully blossomed boundless wisdom.
Encircling him, on the eight petals of the lotus, are the maṇḍala deities:

To the east Mañjuśrīvīra, white in color.
To the south Vāgīśvara, brilliant orange.
To the west Vādirāṭ, red in color.
To the north Vajratīkṣṇa, a dark blazing blue.

Each of them holds the sword of wisdom and a scripture.
They are adorned with silks and jeweled ornaments and sit in vajra posture.
To the southeast is Vajra Sarasvatī, the color of moonlight.
To the southwest is Jewel Sarasvatī, brilliant yellow.

To the northwest is Lotus Sarasvatī, red in color.
To the northeast is Action Sarasvatī, deep green in color.
Each of them holds a jeweled lute in her two hands.
They are perfected with silks and jeweled ornaments, and sit cross-legged with knees slightly upraised.

At the four gates are the four great kings.
Filling the space in between, an ocean of the three roots gathers like clouds.
These forms of illusory wisdom, the unity of appearance and emptiness,

Are spontaneously present as the essence of the three vajras,
And are perfected with the supreme empowerment of the five wisdom families.

OṂ ĀḤ HŪṂ
OṂ HŪṂ TRAṂ HRĪḤ ĀḤ
ABHIṢIÑCA HŪṂ

For the invitation, say:

HŪṂ HRĪḤ
From the supreme emanated celestial realm, Lotus Net,
On the southwestern continent called Cāmara
Knowledge holder Vādisiṃha, the indivisibility of the three bodies,
Together with your retinue, a limitless ocean of the three roots,

With deep longing I invite you to this place of devotion.
Please come due to your compassionate vow,
Dispel all obstacles and grant the supreme and common accomplishments!

OṂ ĀḤ HŪṂ VAJRA GURU PADMA TÖTRENG TSAL VAJRA SAMAYA DZAḤ SIDDHI PHALA HŪṂ ĀḤ
DZAḤ HŪṂ BAṂ HOḤ
SAMAYA TIṢTHA LHAN

Saying this, the samaya being and wisdom being are joined.

To pay homage, say:

HŪṂ HRĪḤ
Without arising, ceasing, or changing, you perfect all activity.
Your naturally arisen compassion liberates all beings.
Like a wish-fulfilling jewel, you bring down a rain of accomplishments.
I pay homage to Vādisiṃha and your retinue!

ATI PŪ HOḤ
PRATIŚA HOḤ

For the offering say:

OṂ ĀḤ HŪṂ
I offer the outer offerings, an ocean of sense pleasures, gathered like clouds;
The inner offerings, inconceivable medicine, rakta and torma;
The secret offerings, the unity of bliss and emptiness, the space of wisdom.
Accepting these, please bestow the supreme and common accomplishments!

OṂ VAJRA ARGHAM PADYAM PUṢPE DHŪPE ĀLOKE GANDHE NAIVEDYE ŚABDA SARVA PAÑCA RAKTA BALIṂTA MAHĀ PŪJĀ ĀḤ HŪṂ

For the praises say:

OṂ
Fully blossomed splendor of the light of supreme knowledge and wisdom,
Lord of knowledge holders, having left birth and death behind.
To the great paṇḍita of Yangleshö, Vādisiṃha,
Who is victorious over all opponents, I offer homage and praise!

Only father of the victorious ones of the three times, Mañjuśrī,
Mother from whom all victors take birth, goddess Sarasvatī,
The display of the four families that tame all beings, the illusory net,
To the perfect splendor of the maṇḍala, I offer homage and praise!

For the recitation, first arouse the deities for the recitation by saying:

HŪṂ HRĪḤ
Deities who play as illusory wisdom
In this essential maṇḍala of awakened mind
Joyfully recall your unbreakable vajra samaya
And bestow blessings, empowerment, and accomplishments!

For the mantra recitation of the main deity say:

At the heart center of the knowledge holder Vādisiṃha
On a moon disc, the mantra garland encircles HRĪḤ.
Light rays shine forth, clearing the dark ignorance of all beings.
The wisdom of the victors and their heirs,
And the intelligence of all noble listeners, solitary realizers, and ordinary beings
Takes the form of light and is gathered, dissolving into oneself.
The light of supreme knowledge and wisdom unfolds.

Say this and practice samādhi—the basis of which is the clarity, stable confidence, and recollection of purity of the deity—keeping your mind one-pointedly focused.

OṂ ĀḤ HŪṂ VAJRA GURU PADMA PRAJÑĀ JÑANĀ SARVA SIDDHI HŪṂ

Recite this until you reach the appropriate number of recitations for the principal deity. If you wish to proceed with the recitation for the retinue, the general visualization is as follows.

At the heart center of the four families of Mañjuśrī on a moon disc is DHĪḤ
At the heart center of the four families of Sarasvatī on a sun disc is HRĪḤ
Encircled by a mantra garland of his or her own color.
Light rays from the heart of the main deity inspire their minds, and
Light rays shine forth clearing the dark ignorance of all beings . . .

And so forth, follow the visualization as above.

For White Mañjuśrī:

OṂ VAC YEDAM NAMA

For Vāgīśvara:

OṂ VĀGĪŚVARI MUM

For Red Mañjuśrī:

OṂ HRĪḤ DHĪḤ MAME DĪPAM MAÑJUŚRĪ MUM HRĪḤ PRAJÑĀ VARDHANI HRĪḤ DHĪḤ SVĀHĀ

For Vajratīkṣṇa:

OṂ MAÑJUŚRĪ VAJRATĪKṢṆA HARA HŪṂ PHAṬ

For White Sarasvatī:

HRĪṂ HRĪṂ HRĪṂ

For Yellow Sarasvatī:

OṂ SARASVATYAI MAHĀ MEDHI TIṢTHA KURU HŪṂ

For Red Sarasvatī:

OṂ SARASVATYAI HRĪḤ HRĪḤ HRĪḤ

For Green Sarasvatī:

OṂ PICU PICU PRAJÑĀ VARDHANI JVALA JVALA MEDHI VARDHANI DHĪḤRI DHĪḤRI BUDDHI VARDHANI SVĀHĀ

Recite these as much as you are able, or if you wish to be skilled in composition, strive to recite more of White Mañjuśrī's mantras. At the end of the session, join your palms and supplicate like this:

OṂ
The single embodiment of the superior knowledge and wisdom
Of the victorious ones and their heirs in all three times,
The supreme great lord of all families,
Guru Vādisiṃha,

Indivisible from Mañjuśrī and Sarasvatī,
Deities of the illusory net of means and knowledge,
Lord and your retinue of emanations,
Please pay me heed!

Bless me with your great compassion,
That the light of wisdom may fully blossom,
That I may attain perfect recollection, memory, clairvoyance,
and samādhi
Spontaneously and without effort!

From now until I reach enlightenment
Knowledge holder, Guru Mañjuśrī,
Please act as my spiritual guide.
May I swiftly attain omniscient wisdom!

Say this and also recite the vowels and consonants, and so forth, as an amendment; make brief offerings and praises; and recite the hundred-syllable mantra to confess your mistakes.

HŪṂ HŪṂ HŪṂ
The maṇḍala of the world and beings dissolves into me,
And I dissolve into the life-force HRĪḤ
This also dissolves into the radiance of luminosity,
beyond observation.

PHAṬ PHAṬ PHAṬ
It arises again as the pure maṇḍala.

Say this as you enter into and emerge from luminosity. Dedicate the virtue and recite verses of auspiciousness as usual, or say:

HOḤ
Through having accomplished the maṇḍala of Vādisiṃha
May I and all limitless sentient beings
Spontaneously accomplish the four activities
And be liberated into the expanse of the dharma body!

May the blessings of the root and lineage gurus enter in my heart!
May the yidam deities and ḍākinīs follow my body like my shadow!
May the dharma protectors and guardians clear away all obstacles!
May there be the auspiciousness of attaining the supreme and common accomplishments!

Put forth effort to engage in the practice in this way. The number of recitations for practicing in this manner is not clearly stated. However, with respect to the time and the signs of accomplishment, the text itself says:

> *It only takes between one month and half a year before one directly beholds the faces of the guru and his retinue of Mañjuśrī and Sarasvatī, hears the sound of their mantras, and gives birth to samādhi and wisdom. In dreams one will receive signs, such as discovering representations of enlightened body, speech, and mind, watching the rise of the sun and moon, encountering flowers and fruits, large rivers expanding, and fires blazing. Thus, one's intelligence will improve.*

Bibliography

Dilgo Khyentse. *Pure Appearance*. Halifax: Nalanda Translation Committee, 2002.

Doctor, Andreas. *Tibetan Treasure Literature*. Ithaca, N.Y.: Snow Lion Publications, 2005.

Dudjom Rinpoche. *The Nyingma School of Tibetan Buddhism: Its Fundamentals and History*. 2 vols. Translated by Gyurme Dorje and Matthew Kapstein. Boston: Wisdom Publications, 1991.

Jamgön Kongtrul Lodrö Thaye. *Creation and Completion: Essential Points of Tantric Meditation*. Translated by Sarah Harding. Boston: Wisdom Publications, 1996.

Jamgön Mipham. *Luminous Essence: A Guide to the Guhyagarbha Tantra*. Translated by Dharmachakra Translation Committee. Ithaca, N.Y.: Snow Lion Publications, 2009.

Jigme Lingpa Patrul Rinpoche, and Getse Mahāpaṇḍita. *Deity, Mantra, and Wisdom: Development Stage Meditation in Tibetan Buddhist Tantra*. Translated by Dharmachakra Translation Committee. Ithaca, N.Y.: Snow Lion Publications, 2007.

Khenpo Namdrol. *The Practice of Vajrakilaya*. Ithaca, N.Y.: Snow Lion Publications, 1999.

Köppl, Heidi. *Establishing Appearances as Divine*. Ithaca, N.Y.: Snow Lion Publications, 2008.

Kunsang, Erik Pema. *Blooming Intelligence: The Practice of Guru Mawey Senge, The Lion of Speech, according to the Tukdrup Barchey Künsel.* Kathmandu, Nepal: Rangjung Yeshe Publications, 1995.

Kunsang, Erik Pema, and Marcia Binder Schmidt. *Blazing Splendor: The Memoirs of Tulku Urgyen Rinpoche.* Hong Kong: Rangjung Yeshe Publications, 2005.

Padmasambhava. *Advice from the Lotus-Born: A Collection of Padmasambhava's Advice to the Dakini Yeshe Tsogyal and Other Close Disciples.* Translated by Erik Hein Schmidt. Kathmandu, Nepal: Rangjung Yeshe Publications, 1996.

———. *Dakini Teachings.* Translated by Erik Hein Schmidt. Kathmandu, Nepal: Rangjung Yeshe Publications, 1999.

Padmasambhava, and Jamgön Kongtrül the Great. *The Light of Wisdom.* Vol. 2. Translated by Erik Hein Schmidt. Kathmandu, Nepal: Rangjung Yeshe Publications, 1986.

Thondup, Tulku. *Hidden Teachings of Tibet: An Explanation of the Terma Tradition of the Nyingma School of Buddhism.* London: Wisdom Publications, 1986.